MW00365803

<u>*My Act of Worship*</u>

*"The Cry of My Heart, The Hope of My Faith,
And His Response to it All!"*

By Jason Gallimore

DEDICATION

"Most importantly, I write to worship You. I write to speak about what I know to be true and what I believe to be true. I hope to honor and glorify You with my words. I pray if there is anything You want said, please help me to accurately capture it and portray it. I am Your servant first and foremost, even when I am unsure of how to serve. My writings are my treasured way to draw near to You."

-Jason Gallimore

CONTENTS

BETWEEN THE LINES

*T*he Cry of My Heart, The Hope of my Faith, and His Response to it All *(My Heart; My Hope; His Reply)* is designed to trigger personal connections. Each writing is a standalone reflection written to an unknown person in their time of need. Although not every emotion expressed by the narrator is felt all the time by everyone, I believe someone, somewhere, will identify with its characterization. My hope is to reach them and show them *God's* beautiful, bountiful love! Maybe these writings will mend a broken heart. Maybe they will lift a weary spirit. Maybe they will rescue a dying faith. In any case, I hope they forever impact the reader, shining *Heaven's Light* into the darkness. And if even one life is positively affected by this message of hope, then this book has served its intended purpose.

Some pieces reflect me in part. Yet in others, I project how I would feel if I were that person living in the environment I'm describing within the work. Generally speaking, each is a representation of a fictional character who receives a nonfictional message of *God's Truth*. Again, the beauty of *God* is *His* message is true today, tomorrow and yesterday; it is not relative. *His Truth* pertains to *ALL*, and *ALL* can perceive it.

The book is laid out with central themes of *"Truth and Worship," "Mercy and Grace," "Peace and Hope," "Trust and Faith,"* and *"Direction and Surrender"* to guide the reader. Each writing falls into one of these perspectives. I think as we travel throughout life, there are times when each category is necessary. The purpose of this collection of writings into a book is to help you when you find yourself facing a question; stopped at a crossroads; or just wanting to celebrate. Some writings are poetic, some are more rhythmic, others are not. There is a message in each, and each has a purpose. The writing style is simply the way that message materialized, finding its way out of my head and onto paper.

This is not a devotional, but an inspirational. Take the time to read it. Reflect on it. Return to it. Rely on it as long as you need its message of truth – most importantly though, don't forget it! My only suggestion would be not to read this in one or two or three ... (I think you get my point) sittings. These truths are deeper than what you can gleam from skimming the surface. Allow the messages to penetrate and resonate. Allow yourself to be swept up into the emotion of the character who is telling their story. I'm sure you will relate, and after doing so, bring your particular reality to *God* for closer examination and conversation. Take a spiritual walk with *God*, drawing near to *Him* by using these writings as markers along your path.

THE STORY BEHIND THE STORIES

*S*o, what does it mean to listen to *God*? I know for each of us, *He* communicates just a little bit differently, and for me, *He* caught my attention in a way I didn't anticipate.

...It was 1:30am on a summer morning in 2007. As you would expect, everyone in my home was asleep, but I was in the basement reading. I'm not a big reader, but this book was captivating – I couldn't put down. It was a book on Apologetics, a subject I'd found fascinating. I was intrigued, stimulated by all the evidence to support my faith. You might say, my mind was 'ripe' with thought but I didn't have any particular thoughts. Do you know what I mean? It was a strange moment where I knew I wanted to capture "the moment," but I didn't know how-to or why.

My anticipation was swelling. Anticipation of what, I couldn't' say. But I was not tired, and I felt an inexplicable urge to write something. In fact, I'd go a step further and say I felt compelled to write something. Write about what – I had no idea! Regardless, the laptop, sitting in front of me on the desk was calling out my name, practically begging me to open it and begin. In an awkward moment of responding to "the moment," I opened the computer to a new Word document, and I waited to see what would unfold.

I sat quiet for just a moment, and then began to type whatever came to my mind. The words practically raced across the page – a sentence turned into more and more. A few short hours later, I had finished my very first writing and it was an eye-opening pronouncement of truth, wrapped nicely in a message of hope and purpose. It was a clear message about *God's* love and our importance to *Him*.

In this relatively brief time, I learned a truth about *God* and about me. This truth was something that had now been woven into my heart during the literal writing process. It was a truth that reinforced other truths, which I had been taught in years past. It was a plain truth but a poignant and impactful one. It made clear to me that *God* cared about me specifically and that I was special. I was more than "Just a Man" – and the beauty of this message was it wasn't for me alone. We are *ALL* more. Our significance is in *Who* we are, not *What* we are!

Ironically, after I finished writing and had some time to ponder, I began to process "the process." In the past, writing was never something I had done just for fun. Sure, I had written essays and papers, short stories and speeches throughout high school and college, but they always had clear purpose and direction from the outset. This time however, it was all-together different. I felt the same drive to write but lacked any outlined guidance. And although I had hit every keystroke, I couldn't take credit for any of this writing. Yes, there was only me in the room, but I was not the only one there! I truly believe *God* had written this piece and I was merely the instrument.

No, *He* didn't write it literally or supernaturally, but

more used me like a surrogate. *He* provided the thoughts, and I placed them on the page. Just like a director who guides the movie crew and actors, *He* saw the big picture in *His* mind, and *He* inserted those thoughts into mine. Together we hammered out the paragraphs and the details – *His* thoughts, *His* message, my hands. I realistically did no more than just be present.

And to prove this point, I've tried to replicate that moment on every other writing since! I can sincerely attest it has never been as simple as it was that early summer morning. The words have never flowed quite the same. But again, since I have had time to reflect on the process, I'm convinced it was not supposed to be that simple or easy anyways.

The first writing was designed to help encourage me by acting as a springboard into a "writer's walk" with *God* – a journey where we spend time together and contemplate concepts and conclusions. *He* wants me to ponder, process, listen, look, and be present to *His* message in *His* timing. *He* then includes me in capturing those thoughts. I've found I'm asked to listen more than write and I believe this has helped me to pause and be patient, allowing me to "hear" *God's Truth* through all of the distracting background noises in a busy life. This type of soul-searching has asked me to be deliberate in my walk with *God*. It has helped me to seek *God* and search for *Him*.

After thirteen years of writing in this manner, I've reached this undeniable realization: Writing was not something that was ever supposed to be easy, merely something that was supposed to be deliberate and meaningful, where faith and intention intersect to create a solid foundation of trust. If writing had been a simple and easy expression of my faith, I never would have grown spiritually, and I probably wouldn't have been driven to continue to write more than a decade later.

This methodology is exactly how I've discovered *God* works with others in their acts and expressions of worship. *God* asks us all to be still and listen to *Him*. Often, it's a still small voice that we hear. *Was God in the whirlwind? Was God in the fire? Was God in the Earthquake? Was God in the cave? Yes, He was everywhere!* But *He* was also in the whispers, and a whisper is what I have learned to listen for.

The purpose of these writings was always simple – to listen – listen to what *God* was placing on my mind and heart and portray it to the best of my ability on paper. One after the other, year after year, this was my focus each time I sat down to write. I tried to listen to the *Holy Spirit's* guidance and preserve those thoughts with pen to page. Often, I did not know what the piece would even resemble until it was nearly finished. It was truly a practice in exploratory writing where *God* revealed a truth that I didn't foresee coming. My job was just to be patient and make time for *Him* – *He* took care of the rest.

I poured over each work, revisiting and rewriting, praying and pausing until I felt like each individual line was as it was intended. It was always a work in progress, and even when I thought I was finished, I'd find one word or punctuation that needed revision. The goal was to capture the essence as precisely as I could – and let me tell you, that takes time. After all was said and done though, I felt like it was not hard; but in truth, it was not easy either. Hopefully one day you too will find yourself sitting in front of a closed laptop with a compelling drive to write something. And if so, I'd encourage you to open the lid and begin your journey! You won't regret it!

"Why Me? Why Now?"

I've had people ask what makes me someone they should listen to? Why am I authoring a book? Frankly, nothing makes me worthy to listen to! Again, I don't claim to write these as much as I try to listen to *God* and transpose *His* message of truth and love. I give *Him* all the glory. I humbly and wholly recognize *His* workings. It's only when *God* moved that things happened. No, I am not claiming to be a prophet or someone *God* speaks to audibly. I do believe though, if you are intentionally trying, you can discern the *Holy Spirit's* nudging and directing – and in each of these cases, I know *God* guided me with words *He* wanted shared.

I once remember hearing a sermon rendered by Chuck Swindol on his ministry *"Insight for Living"* where during the message, Chuck said something that resonated above all the other sounds in the room. *"It's not about the man, but the message..."* That phrase stopped me in my tracks. Literally this is what I am saying here – none of these writings should reflect on me in anyway other than they are my "offering" to my *Creator*. They are *"My Act of Worship!"*

As a former police officer and now firefighter, I've seen the toll that despair takes on mankind. Under the glow of red and blue lights, I've witnessed firsthand broken people. Suicide is at the highest it has ever been; violence is rampant in every corner of the earth; death is all too familiar for families and friends; sickness is a daily occurrence; addiction is a devilish detail people routinely struggle to keep hidden; and pain is sadly very, very real. I am more convinced than ever for the need of *God's Truth* – we all need *His* hope!

The challenge we perpetually seem to face is that we want to overcome these heartbreaks of life, but we don't have the medicine or the cure. Perhaps more accurately stated, we don't have a compass or solid foundation to build upon. People are so afraid to admit their imperfection that they won't allow for the perfect, healing hands of *God* to unbind them and heal their land. They ignore truth to cover-up their insecurity. This collection of writings is intended to provide you with that hope of *God Almighty*. Yes, people are desperate, but *Hope* springs eternal!

So, let me finish this book's introduction with a question, *"How Important is it to know how God feels about you?"* – No not "you" in theory or "you" as a generality, but *"YOU!"* personally? Well, open-up the pages and find out...

SECTIONAL CHARACTERISTICS

*A*rranged as a compilation, this book is a series of inspirational writings each articulating a unique facet of *God's* loving character. The sectionals present vivid portrayals of authentic self-discoveries, where sincere questions are raised and contrasted against genuine replies from a divine essence. The human heart is full of unchained emotion, and these pieces expose those varied sentiments as they accompany a person through daily living.

In this book, the reader will recognize they are not alone either in relation to their fellow man or relationship with their loving *God*. Anyone who has been challenged by disappointment and confusion regarding the question of *"why?"* will find comfort between these pages. Anyone who has questioned their self-worth will find value in their very existence. Anyone who has wondered about *God's* supernatural capacity will find calculation and majesty in *His* earthly creations.

Although the writings unfold across varying backdrops, eliciting a profound and deep central devotion to *God Almighty* and *His Son Jesus Christ*, they each can be authentically arranged into more derived sections of *"Truth and Worship," "Mercy and Grace," "Peace and Hope," "Trust and Faith,"* and *"Direction and Surrender."* I sincerely believe at some point you will find windows into your very life through each of these sectionals – if not today, maybe tomorrow or next year, but at some point, you too will say, "I've been there!"

And this is the beauty of the calculated human experience that *God* has created. We are not alone, neither in our struggles nor our support from loving brothers and sisters who have walked a mile in our shoes – making it out to the other side. As life continues to hurl obstacles your way, you will have a renewed, *Heavenly-centered* perspective allowing you to see past the temporary distractions and focus on the big picture, living with eternity in the forefront of your mind.

Feel free to skip around from one section to another – these are not chronological in their nature. Dive into the writings as they were intended to be read, bookmarking the storms of life as they emerge with *God's* eternal perspectives. Place these words of truth into your mind at the exact time they are needed most. <u>*My Act of Worship: "The Cry of My Heart, The Hope of My Faith, and His Response to It All"*</u> is as much a discovery of *God's Truth* as it is a reinforcement of it. Please use this book according to your need and its design!

1

TRUTH AND WORSHIP

ruth and Worship is dedicated to reminding us of God's excellence, might, and love. The pieces detail *God's* authentic power in creation, *His* love in salvation, and *His Son* in significance. The intention in this grouping is to not draw a connection to an individual as much as to connect humanity with its *King*. Whether it is through recognizing profound truth or holy worship, this section fixes our gaze upon *Our Creator*.

Just a Man
Your Story
A Portrait of Love
The Significance of One
The Carpenter of Heaven and Earth
That Day
The Greatness of 'I AM'
You Stand Alone
The Creator
Beautiful to Your Ears
And the Truth Is!
My Song of Love

JUST A MAN

I am not special; I am just a man. Not a scholar, but simple and sincere. I struggle daily to walk the line, trying to fight against an oncoming and ongoing world. I slip, I fall, and I get up, only to fall again. Sometimes I try not to. Sometimes I look to. Either way, the fall is inevitable. My collapse leaves me disappointed, distressed, and disoriented. Sometimes I don't know I have even been tripped up until I look around and detect my scattered self. Frustration surrounds me. How can I survive by stumbling my way throughout life? That road is too tiresome, and I am weary. I am just a man.

It is a battle to stay upright. What if in weakness I surrender? What if I cannot hold up under the weight? Unease begins to encircle me. It seems unfair that at birth I unknowingly wandered outside the womb and encountered this condition. I stepped immediately onto foreign soil and was not welcome. Not only do I face a self-concerning humanity, but I learned an enemy existed who watches and waits for me. He is patient, content to stalk, looking for an opportunity to seize. I know he is there, approaching in time. Whether directly or casually, I can be sure the assault is underway. What's more, I recognize I am vulnerable. How can I win? I am not a warrior, I am just a man.

Fear has entangled me. Just when I think I cannot withstand, I am quietly reminded with the softness of a whisper there is *One* who knows my angst, *One* who knows my adversary, *One* who knows my name, and *One* who cares to see me triumph. Quickly I cry out, and out of the darkness *He* comes. Like a light piercing the night, *He* finds me and collects me in *His* palm. *He* carries me as a child in his father's arms. I rest. I cannot help it. I am exhausted. I am just a man.

My spirit transformed, my fears now gone, my weight lifted, I am finally at peace. *He* returns me to *His* treasure chest like a beloved and fragile family jewel, handed down through time. What did I do to deserve this rescue but ask? When did I become a prized possession, I am just a man?

How great are the rewards of this fresh existence! Eternal life has been granted. My soul is *Heavenly* bound. What marvelous freedom this renewed life offers! Before I was lost, but now I have been found, and once found, never to be lost again. Now I live, I love, and I let go. I know I will still fall, but I am unafraid. *He* is there to catch me. Thank *God* I am not alone. Thank *God*, I am not just a man!

YOUR STORY

*Y*our story is my story, and this has always been. From the beginning our paths were united, forged by a bond time could never bend. While still in darkness, where emptiness did surround. My thoughts of you sparkled. In the absence, your essence twinkled all around. I could see your face. I could hear your heartbeat. I could touch your very soul. I knew everything that would be about you, for you were my child long before you were even born. And though your pages were yet to be written, not one would ever be blank because you were always my heart's purpose and intention.

Your story is my story with every step of every day. There is never a moment that I am ever far away. I'm nearby in the evening, when nightfall calls your burdens undone. And I welcome you warmly in the morning, when those shadows make their frantic run. I listen anxiously for your laugh. I feel deep hurt from your pain. I cry genuine tears when you weep, and I smile proudly that you pray. For you are my beloved, set apart as my very own. From my throne room I watch you closely. My child you don't walk alone. And with each new hour that passes, know your minutes are not something to dread. Rather, your story is a masterpiece simply waiting to be read!

Your story is my story even when the words don't sound quite right. And your journey takes a turn, twisting unexpectedly out of sight. It's times like these where fear will try to make its home. Desperation will knock, and panic will unlock the door. But look past this worry. *My Love*, weary no more! None of what happens to you is beyond my might or exceeds the power I bestow. For *I AM* today, as I will be tomorrow and forever the same. Rejoice, I will come again! Stand firm and reclaim this day!

Your story is my story, right-up to your last breath. When all the sands have fallen, and the hourglass has not one grain left. Yes, your life on earth is over, and your circle drawn to a close. Death no longer patient for its bounty, but ready to collect that which it is owed. Your story may feel like it's finished and the last act a *Fait Accompli*. But don't be deceived by the stage's descending curtain. A new chapter is awaiting, flip the page, let's begin!

Your story is my story and where I am you too will be. For I have prepared you a place to dwell, alongside of me for an eternity. Those gates of *Heaven* swing open; to you they welcome with arms wide. Since your fate was long-ago sealed, the moment you took the hand of my risen *Christ*. My gift of love you accepted, and thus were justly saved. My grace for you sufficient, now you will walk on streets richly paved. And if your story seems surprising, or you find yourself asking "why?" in the end. Just remember while it was being written, it was *I, The Lord God Almighty,* who held its pen. So, with paradise on the horizon, in glory together will we live. My home is your home forever, and this my child, is how it has always been!

A PORTRAIT OF LOVE

*E*very artist has a vision, a dream they must capture and share. There is a picture they feel compelled to bring to light in order for others to know their heart's deepest desires. They yield not until this image has been vividly portrayed and forever preserved, depicting clearly and completely the longings that lie within their soul. They create with a purpose, and to that purpose they are bound.

He is no different. *He* has a blueprint in mind that promises to make visible the invisible, illuminating *His* purest yearnings and displaying *His* divine design. Unlike some however, *His* mission is not one of gloom but of grandeur. *His* will be the greatest of all works, unequivocally beautiful while exclaiming excellence to any who examine it. The universe stands still in wonderment as it watches and waits, pondering what kind of brilliance is in store.

Focused and determined, *He* begins; eager to face the impending challenge and eager to triumph over it.

...*His* fingers brush the canvas lightly and splendor takes shape, transforming the ordinary into extraordinary. Dabs of gentle colors swirl into the air and fall gracefully down to the earth. Red, yellow, white and green – a collage, sprinkled delicately throughout the countryside. Flowers are the initial handiwork of *His* softly bristled stroke. Their petals radiate brightly in the morning dew, and blush quietly in the evening mist. Each one perfectly positioned, perfectly arranged, and perfectly pleasing. Angelic eyes gaze in awe at their magnificence, for they bathe in beauty and cry serenity to any around.

Next, sculpted in dirt and water, from the ash of earthly soil arises the mountains and peaks. They distinctly exhibit a rugged might, majestically towering the landscape. At the touch of *His* hand, they roar into the sky and rage with power. Yet cower and crumble at the sound of *His* command. Against these massive marvels the sun sets, casting a brilliant backdrop and painting the horizon with a radiant glow of assorted hues. All who see these stoned-walled watchtowers bow down in astonishment. They are speechless; so much beauty to behold, so much benevolence to bestow.

Still not content, *He* continues on with *His* piece. *He* sketches into place the rivers, who wind jaggedly alongside the terrain. Tranquility whispers as the water passes by – patiently searching for its home in the sea. It is destined to find it, but never satisfied until it does. *He* shades the river a calming blue to match the sky above and restore peace below. The river will be the lifeblood to *His* natural world, flowing constantly and abundantly; never to fail, never to forget, and never to fade away.

Maintaining *His* pursuit of perfection, *He* proceeds to outline wild fields of exotic vegetation scattered across the land. These meadows are untamed. Nevertheless, they dance harmoniously with the wind, swaying back and forth, rising and falling in unison like a string concerto. Inside their boundaries dwell creatures large and small. They find comfort and security, and most importantly symbiosis within their surroundings. It is a deliberate demonstration of tenderness, mercy, and grace.

Almost complete, *He* has one final, vital element to etch. Squarely in the middle, amongst all the beauty and majesty, *He* centers *His* attention. This will be the focal point of *His* composition; the inspiration behind the incandescent image *He* has been so diligently crafting. *His* palm glides elegantly over the cloth, and slowly *His* intention becomes evident. It is a reflection of himself; not fully expressed, but a representation nonetheless. Although *He* is infinite, *He* contains *His* being, confining it to skin and bone. *He* is still invincible, but now also vulnerable. *He* gives this fragile divinity eyes to see, a heart to adore, and most importantly, a saving commission not to be ignored. This man will live to suffer so others will not. *He* is gracious and glorious, and nothing short of *God* incarnate. It is a flawless finish to a breathtaking work of art...

At last, *He* sets *His* instruments aside and looks intently at this portrait. It exquisitely encapsulates exactly what *His* mind's eye had foreseen. Every detail, every rough edge is just as *He* hoped it would be. A true masterpiece. *His* is unlike any before or any to come. All of *Heaven* rejoices as they acknowledge the grandness of *His* creation and the fulfillment of *His* plan. *His* burden is now at ease, *His* yoke now released. To a dying humanity, *He* has given life, love, and loveliness. *He* is well pleased and so *He* rests, proclaiming, "It is good!"

THE SIGNIFICANCE OF ONE

*H*ow significant is one? Is it just a number, or is it something more? Does one live alone, or does it need others to give it value and worth? Is one simply a part of the whole, or is it a whole on its own? Although one can be measured, can it be multiplied? Is one a concrete object, or is one merely a concept; a creative idea; a constructed conclusion? Eventually, will one cease to exist, or has one existed forever? One is certainly a question, but is one an answer?

One can be many things, and many things can be one. One is a goal; one is a dream, a passion and a pursuit. It is a beginning and, in some cases, an end. To be "*The One*" is a hope. To be '*Number One*' is a drive. People chase one with all their heart, sometimes finding one was never *The One* to begin with. One has begun revolutions, and one has revealed revelation. One launches a fortune, and one has won lotteries. One snowflake announces the coming of winter, and one raindrop has released a flood. One spark can ignite a fire and one decision can alter a future. One traitor can end a cause and one word can inspire a nation.

Among men, a man is no different. One man can forever change the course of history. But men, sadly, are insignificant, here today and gone tomorrow. Throughout time, a single man has left his mark and altered the direction of the human race. Whereas men will just follow the flock, like sheep to the slaughter, blindly walking towards the end, never knowing their steps and days are numbered: one for one. Men will continue on without giving a second thought to their destination, but a man will often pause for reflection and redirection. Men will come and go, while a man can rise above time and space, transforming the world around him.

Despite the many "ones" to have lived, there is one who uniquely and unequivocally separated himself from all others. *He* is unlike any to come before or to come after. *He* leaves an undying legacy, which defies mortality and transcends time. Although many ones have left an impression, *This One's* imprint will endure throughout the ages.

In the beginning, one fallen angel deviously plotted in darkness to destroy all that was good and holy. However, because of *This One*, light shown into the bleak and black world, creating life and giving hope. Consequently, because of the selfish desires of one defiant man, all men were born into sin. Thankfully, because of *This One's* spotless life of devotion, all men can be forgiven and found innocent on their day of judgment. Sadly, through the words of one impotent leader, death by crucifixion was ordered. Yet gracefully, by the words of *This One*, a dying thief's last request was honored, and an eternal purpose was fully fulfilled. Tragically, at the hands of one soldier, a wounded and broken body was left hanging on a rugged, wooden cross. Astonishingly though, by the power of *This One*, wounded relationships are healed, and humbled broken men will be resurrected. Shamefully, through blinded faith, one coward's final act of greed betrayed a divine cause and seemingly crippled a movement. But gloriously, because of the perfect commitment of *This One*, an empty garment, lying in an empty tomb was all that remained of a failed attempt to rid the world of the loving, living *Lamb of God*.

Without *This One*, life would be futile, and all humanity would be rendered to never-ending damnation. However, by the grace of *God* alone, a passion was personified, and a manger held a *Messiah*. *This One*, who knew the plan – salvation accompanied by suffering – willingly offered *His* life as a sacrifice to save sinners. A ransom for the restless. *He* paid the full price in death so the cost of life would be free. By *His* blood, the wretched were made righteous. *He* made a way through the wilderness to guide the hopeless and undeserving to the doorstep of grace and glory.

To all who seek, *His* way is straight, and *He* shows the direct path to bridge the gap between themselves and the *God of the Universe*. Whether it is the natural or supernatural world, *He* is in complete control. Every knee will bow, and every tongue will confess that *He* is *Lord* and *King*. Justice was *His* mission, and redemption is *His* reward. *He* prepares the heart of man for the plight of living and the honor of *Heaven*. *He* is *The Rock*, and *He* is *The Living Water*. *He* is *The Bride*, and *He* is *The Groom*. But most importantly, *He* is alive, and *His* name is *Jesus*.

How significant is one? The answer is remarkably clear! The significance of one lies solely in what significance the one left behind. Fortunately, with *This One*, there is no doubt. *He* forever changed the future of mankind by redeeming the lost and lonely to a right standing with *God*, ultimately allowing *God*, to finally be *"One"* with *His* beloved creation.

THE CARPENTER OF HEAVEN
AND EARTH

*S*killed in ways beyond measure, the excellence of *His* work speaks loudly without any hesitation. Using thunder as *His* trumpet and lightning the exclamation, *He* crafts such wonders of breathtaking splendor. *He* is the creator; the builder; the designer of all expression. By *His* very word, life took on form. Carving existence into eternity's foundation. *He* is *The Carpenter of Heaven and Earth*, and *He* stands alone, having no rival, equal, or worthy comparison.

With the universe at *His* direction, the world is under *His* construction. Just look around, observe the handiwork of the divine! *His* fingerprints are everywhere, interlaced throughout time. *His* signature is bold; it is easy to find. An artist, with a knack to describe. *He* uses light and darkness, shadow and shine. Nothing is out of *His* reach, nor apart from *His* design. *He* is *The Carpenter of Heaven and Earth*, and not a single space is untouched by *His* hand or unseen by *His* eye.

This architect, who has no deficit or limitation, is the truest definition of expertise and holy perfection. With delicate precision *He* shapes, and with firm understanding *He* molds. The rough edges, they are purposeful, capturing the coarseness of our fight. And the soft lines, intentional, scaled specifically to depict an end to strife. The fire is deliberate and refining, yet the result – undeniably defining. *He* is *The Carpenter of Heaven and Earth*, and the significance of our lives is not an accident to be merely reconciled, or simplistically denied.

While there is so much beauty for each of us to behold, there is still too much brilliance for anyone to fully know. For who can grasp that which they cannot rightly contain or willfully let go? Yes, *He* is *The Carpenter of Heaven and Earth*, and *He* is to be worshipped from the highest high to the lowest low.

And although *His* greatness far surpasses what we could ever imagine or correctly contemplate, *His* loving presence is much, much closer than we would even think. Look high into the sky, and you will see a cosmic demonstration of *His* boundless capabilities. Look nearer to the ground, and you will witness a wide array of *His* colorful creativity. Look deeply within and you will no doubt see *His* own reflection – looking back and smiling! For *He* is *The Carpenter of Heaven and Earth*, and you were made in *His* image, in fact handwoven!

THAT DAY

That Day started out the same as any would. It began early for some and, for others, later. For many, it seemed routine and, for a few, it appeared fresh and full of promise. It showed no sign of storm on the horizon, or signal of savagery in the air. For most, it just came and went the way of every day. Little did anyone know of the real travesty that day would dispatch, or, what's more, of the splendor that would soon be in store. Truth be told, it was impossible to predict the impact *That Day* would have throughout the ripples of time – past, present and future.

That Day's events, surprisingly, started long before the midnight hour. Plotting had been underway since the moment greed and glamour were compromised. A man full of charm and full of character had challenged the conventional wisdom, and for it, he was expected to pay. His teachings were bold and brash, testing the true intentions of the heart, unmasking the motives of the mind and questioning the conscience of all. In addition, to those claiming to follow *God*, his charge was clear. Their lives should reflect proof of that pursuit. His mission was a commission rendered by a higher power – genuine love for thy neighbor and love for *Thy Maker*.

That Day, despite the divine nature of his work and authenticity of his word, anger and resentment arose. Zealots became jealous, and destruction became their demand. This man of *God*, who did no wrong, saw his demise at the hands of a conflicted crowd shouting for him to be crucified. A brutal and belittling death, reserved for the wicked, had been unleashed on the righteous. And this man was nailed to a wooden cross as the angry looked on. He hung for hours, tirelessly clinging to life, slowly suffocating and painfully passing from this world to the next.

That Day yielded tormenting torture, agonizing abuse, and horrific hostility. It produced confusion and chaos, lasting from morning 'til after midday, never relenting, never relinquishing.

That Day's cruelty brought out hate. It brought out brutality. It brought out the worst in men. It was intended to cripple a cause and end a movement just to appease the pompous and powerful, who were perverting the true law of *God*. Their hope was to retain influence and supremacy. Ironically though, justice was in fact delivered at the hands of the unjust, and on *That Day*, the best of *God* was displayed for all the world to witness.

That Day that seemed to never end, did end, but not in loss, rather in triumph. Satan's final attempt to reclaim victory was washed away by the very blood he shed. The pain that was felt was felt for a purpose. The plan required a lamb, and the people needed a lion. On *That Day*, they got both! A prophesy from prophets of old foretold of *That Day* and its carnage, but they also forecasted a resurrection three days later. The grave would be robbed of its occupant and death would be exchanged for life. Faithfully, *God* fulfilled his pledge, and the tomb where that man lay, lies empty. Furthermore, like the *Christ*, *God* made a way through the wilderness for others to follow and share in this glorious delight. The only condition, sinners must accept this state and their gift will be eternal bliss.

Although on *That Day*, brutality is often thought of, beauty should not be missed. Without *That Day*, life would be hopeless; life would be lost. Without *That Day*, a pardon would not be granted and the guilty would still stand accused, rightfully so, sentenced to eternal damnation. Without *That Day*, hope would be hidden, and the heart of the *Father* would be broken. Without *That Day*, man would be just a moment in time and not a cherished treasure in *Heaven*. Truthfully, on *That Day* much was lost, but thankfully, on *That Day* much, much more was gained.

THE GREATNESS OF 'I AM'

*W*ords cannot describe the greatness of *'I AM'*, for *His* might exceeds that of any man's. And *His* wisdom far surpasses what we can possibly imagine, or even understand. With *His* mind, *He* alone formed the seas and the land. By *His* outstretched hands, *He* rescued the souls of the lost, saving the damned. There are no limitations to what *He* can do, because all *His* ways are trustworthy and *His* will is true. No, words cannot describe the greatness of *'I AM'*!

When light shattered the darkness, and when one heartbeat pounded inside its first chest, *He* was there. When waters stood on end, and when fire was forbidden to singe, *He* was there. When giants fell in defeat, and when the lame stood triumphantly to their feet, *He* was there. When whispers to the wind did calm, and when a procession of believers paraded upon a street of palm, *He* was there. When the condemned man made not a sound, and when a broken body from a wooden cross was lowered down, *He* was there. When death's grip finally would hold no more, and when life's abundance was faithfully and fully restored,

He was there. No, words cannot describe the greatness of *'I AM'*!

Where the nobility of a lion meets the humility of a lamb, *He* can be found. Where a crown of gold is exchanged for one of thorns, *He* can be found. Where the forgiveness of a father outruns the shame of a son, *He* can be found. Where the stains of sin are washed away by a river of grace, *He* can be found. Where love and mercy overshadow hate and history, *He* can be found. No, words cannot describe the greatness of *'I AM'*!

Because justice demanded righteousness, *He* offered *His* one and only son for us. And though the price of salvation was steep, *He* spared it not, pouring out *His* blood to cover the cost for each. None can compare and none should ever dare. Since the beginning, which had no beginning, *He* existed in radiance and splendor. And in the end, which has no ending, *He* will be reigning unrivaled, forever. No, words cannot describe the greatness of *'I AM'*!

YOU STAND ALONE

*Y*ou stand alone. Who can compare? In *You*, lies the wisdom of the ages, the power of the universe, and the pledge of eternity. There is none like *You*. Without *Your* divine touch, nothing that is would be. Before *Your* words, only emptiness was known. But *You* spoke and light sparked in utter darkness, casting creation into being and separating life from death. *Your* hands carefully carved the cosmos, and seamlessly set the solar system into place; such a splendor never before seen. *Your* might molded the earth with delicacy and dominion, placing man on center stage as *Your* treasured trophy; such a benevolence never before bestowed. All was well as *You* sat by, ready and waiting. *Your* plan unveiling. **You Were!**

To this day, *You* stand alone at the meshing point of majesty and mercy, eager to help, ready to act, full of unfailing affection. Hope is the message *You* relay. *Your* declaration of love, freedom from death, and life eternal, resounds. *Your* power, *Your* presence exudes excellence. *Your* intelligence and *Your* genius surpass all. *Your* perfection is perfected in *Your* persona. The stars, the atoms, and everything in between exclaim *Your* brilliance and proclaim *Your* rightful place on the throne of glory. *Your* faithfulness never falters. *Your* justice never compromises. ***You Are*!**

From the first Adam to the last, *Your* light will radiate. *Your* words of truth will resonate. They can be trusted. *You* stand alone as the essence of unrivaled relevance. *Your* reign is endless. *Your* power never ceases. *Your* authority is limitless. *Your* mercy is boundless. *Your* love is abounding. Sons and daughters can count on *You*, just as fathers and mothers did. *Your* endless devotion and *Your* undying love demonstrate *Your* unique passion towards *Your* true love – man. The artist is captured by *His* creation. *You* are the *Lord God Almighty*. There has never been another, nor will there ever be any other like *You*. ***Forever, You Will Be*!**

> *I depend on Your promises; I rest through the night because of them. Daily, I look to You for a peaceful spirit. I stumble and am ensnared by the poisons of the heart and the impurities of life. Yet You spare me, offering me redemption and reprieve from my sentence. I surrender to my shaken spirit in the face of failure and frustration. Still You salvage my integrity and raise me up from despair, upholding me in Your righteous right hand. You sustain me and give me provision. The storms of life surge and You restrain the wind; reduce the waves; and calm the water. You are Lord of my life and Lord of all. Your gracious tenderness reassures my fragile heart that in the midst of brokenness, You will make me whole. God, I praise You for You are regardless of What is!*

THE CREATOR

The Creator has created,
and rest assured it was not in vain,
He cares about my struggles
and *He* knows my very name.
Who I am is not a mishap,
who I am is not a mistake,
It's the timeless gift of *God*
to refine the superficial that once made me fake.
He wants my true heart
– the one *He* alone knows is there,
So *He'll* dig and uncover,
rendering it exposed and completely bare.
At that point *He* can transform,
at that point *He* can mold,
Shaping and cradling the child
that *He* himself first bore.

For *He* is *God* of the good, and *He* is *God* of the bad,
He is *God* the happy, and *He* is *God* of the sad.
He is *God* of the then, and *He* is *God* of the now,
He is *God* of the city, and *He* is *God* of the town.
He is *God* of the humble, and *He* is *God* of the proud,
He is *God* of the lost, and *He* is *God* of the found!

BEAUTIFUL TO YOUR EARS

I pray my life is a song beautiful to *Your* ears. One so satisfying, I hope *You* smile when it is what *You* hear. Let my days be focused and my moments be true, capturing the essence of a man devoted to following and serving only *You*. May my words and thoughts be a sweet surreal sound, rising to meet *You* in glory where *Your* angels surround. Create a melody from within my soul that rings out gently, dancing between the towering *Cherubim* and *Seraphim*, harmoniously, and ever so elegantly.

Lord, I am your instrument, *Your* creation. I am the clay *You* sculpted with splendid divination. My hands are *Your* source of giving; my feet are *Your* means of going. Their purpose is to extend *Your* eternal, rewarding, life-saving message. A man's travels can be far, and his adventures a widespread expression. But may I cast the shadow of a man truly drawn-in by a lasting, focused, *Godly* connection. Make my steps delicate when appropriate and distinct where necessary, but always dedicated, moving deliberately towards completion. To where my path will lead, of this I cannot be sure, but I am bound and determined to a purpose of everlasting, transcending transformation. How I get there and when it will all happen, of this *God* only knows. But I am ready, willing, and able, committed to *Your* unspeakable, holy throne.

Who I am today is only a temporary perception – who I want to be forever, that is the real reflection! Construct my conscience and mold my mind, to serenade *You, The Great and Glorious Divine*. Whittle away my weaknesses into beauty pure and unscathed. Compose a magnificent chorus to be loud and boldly played. Shape me into a man as sincere as I have never known before – one who comes humbly to *Your* front step, kneeling at *Your* righteous door. Help me to possess a caring heart portrayed of a strict compassion. Whose efforts and actions carve a canvas of commitment to kindness, love, and deep affection.

For without *You*, benevolence is truly and utterly lost. And hope is a shattered conclusion, like a lonely man just watching his watch. To some, this existence is sufficient and satisfactory. But as for me *Lord*, I don't want my minutes to be wasted on the plain or ordinary. So *God,* I ask, "Please make my lifespan a masterpiece that echoes throughout eternity. One that doesn't merely capture a fleeting instance, but rather imparts a living, lasting, life-song of a legacy."

AND THE TRUTH IS!

"*And the truth is...*" How many times have you heard this expression? (I bet more times than you can count!) It seems everyone knows the truth – or at least what they think is the truth – and because they do, they want you to listen to them. People will claim to know the truth to just about everything, but do they? Can they? Is truth really that obtainable? Truth often gets portrayed by its color – black, white, and gray. But is this too broad a brush with too little paint? Is truth merely an incomplete arrangement, or is it something more transcending? Well in order to answer those questions, we must begin by answering these:

What is truth? How important is discovering it? And what is the significance of God's Truth?

AND THE TRUTH IS... Truth is a concrete object, which provides clarity and direction to any who know it. Truth feeds our very existence by establishing our realms of trust. Without truth, there is nothing to trust-in. Truth defines our reality, so if truth is "true," then it creates a precedent worth aspiring to know and utilize in our everyday daily lives. And, if there is a *God*, then truth and, more importantly "*His Truth*," are essential pillars for every person to grapple with and grasp during their lifetime.

Truth is so valuable that I would contend it is the currency that transcends time and space. It is not restricted by boundaries, borders, or beliefs. Truth is truth regardless of whether you agree with it (i.e. gravity doesn't care what you think of it, it holds fast. Time is constantly ticking whether you are watching a clock or not. Love exists independent of how you feel in the moment). Truth is true, and truth is vitally important for all of us to know! Without truth, life would be like walking in a circle with no reason to get off the path and no reason to ever stop walking. Truth is paramount for living, and if truth isn't worthwhile, then neither is living.

"Are you going where you need to go?" – **It doesn't' matter;** *"Are you listening to the correct voices along your way?"* – **Not important;** *"Is your life even worth living?"* – **WHO CARES!!**

If there is no truth, then we are all destined to be obsolete; and continuing to journey, is a complete waste of time – which, in-and-of itself is a real paradox if truth is in fact irrelevant.

Sadly, when truth is relegated to relativism all questions and answers, especially like those above, are pointless to even ask. What worked today is all that matters for today because tomorrow I will have to discover what works for tomorrow. And to search for something mythical such as "truth," is a fantasy that I don't really have time for... again, if time is something that I think is worth relishing (which it wouldn't be because truth doesn't exist.) If truth does not by its definition define any absolute, then it really is not worth pursuing even to the slightest degree. *For how can truth, if it isn't true, justify its place to anyone as a top priority?* Truthfully, it doesn't!

But, if truth does mean something concrete, then it absolutely is worth knowing, and if you are going to ask any questions, then those three above are really the only ones that ought to rise to the top of your forethought. They become our compass as we walk through our days on earth. They define the meaning of life and living. When knowing truth leads to a life of purpose, wholly redirecting people away from the never-ending circle (and accompanying circus), to an identity of uniqueness and significance that places them on a path to somewhere, it should be mentioned. Better yet, it should be shouted; it should be sought after; it should be shared!

AND THE TRUTH IS... God's Truth is just that! It is that ultimate message to be shared. It provides the nourishment for healthy living and healthy dying. It provides the antidote to depression and depravity. It rescues a shipwrecked, stranded soul. *God's Truth* is so much more than a theoretical, theological exercise, or a philosophical, feel-good free-for-all. I know it's a fact that people across the world are starving. And yes, for many it is because of a lack of physical food. But truthfully, we *ALL* are starving for the *Truth of God*. It is the overly abundant sustenance that singlehandedly sets us free from worry, fear, and the *Devil's* lies and destruction. *God's Truth* is that impactful!

Congruently, the appetite for *God's Truth* is that important! It transcends cognitive understanding and even creates physical sustainment. Without it, we are lost and doomed, dead men and women walking. With it, we have hope; we have life; we have joy everlasting! *God's Truth* is what releases us from the fear of the unknown. *God's Truth* is was suspends us when we are discouraged and falling. *God's Truth* is what anchors us in the most intense storms – keeping us from drifting and drowning. *God's Truth* is what feeds us when all we see is stones. *God's Truth* is what tells us we are loved and never alone. *God's Truth* is what lightens the darkened room. *God's Truth* is what *He* wants all of us to know as we navigate a world of unknowns. *God* cares about us and *He* wants us to know it!

Not only that, but *God* wants us to know *His heart, His love, His will,* and *His ways* too. *God's Truth* is our 'True North' and we should set our own compass aside and fix our gaze upon *His* guidance.

I can hear some of you right now asking a very good question, *"If truth is something which is so profound and critical, harboring absolute and universal rules and regulations, how can any single person reign it in and believe they have a precise handle of it?"* This is a fair question. To that I say, "I can't fully grip every eternal, finite truth. You are correct." A simple man, simply living, is not capable to be "Master of the Universe." But what I will counter with is this: *"We can know broad truths and we can translate them into deeper understanding. We can observe truth through the world around us and we can experience truth through living life. And after having done so, compile it into a truth-rolodex, which we can draw from later when we need to."* This is in fact perceived truth, which is in its most precise form the most authentic truth. Its experiential and validated, having proved itself to be true. So yes, we can know truth! After all, we are made in the image of *God*! We must have the capacity to gather *His Truth* when we are willing to look and listen for it. *Are you willing?*

AND THE TRUTH IS... God is waiting to share *His Truth* with each and everyone of us. *He* is never too far away, nor is *He* absent from any moment. Distance and time are no obstacles for *The Great* Devine! *God* cares for *His* creation and *His* love is ever-abounding. So, don't hesitate to ask the questions – be ready to hear the answers! They won't disappoint! *He* is and always has been that truth – *"The Truth"* – that sets us free.

MY SONG OF LOVE

Oh *God*, I sing to *You*, but I have no words,
My heart is full, and my soul alive,
So, how do I reveal it to *You*?
Love is all that I have.

Love, which *You* have shown me,
Love, which *You* have given me,
Love is how *You* made me,
And love runs, overflowing from my very being.
Imagine how deep and vast it must be.
Imagine how impossible it is to contain.

Yet, my song is full in me.
It encompasses my passions and my pursuits.
I know it pales in comparison,
merely a small glimpse of what *You* are.
But I lay it down before *You* anyway,
Knowing it could never equate.

You are complete and perfect,
Which I am far from.
You are light and glory,
And I am just a man, shame and sin.

My song is sung from my heart, not my tongue.
My wordless song is all I have
So, I raise it holy to *You*.
Oh *God*, I sing to *You*, but I have no words,
All I have is Love.
And, I offer *You*, All I have!

2

MERCY AND GRACE

ercy and Grace makes way for mistakes and clears the path from failure. Plainly, we've all missed the mark; we've "all sinned and fallen short of the glory of *God*". Thankfully, *God* offers forgiveness through *His* son *Jesus Christ*. Without forgiveness, we are lost, but because of *God*'s redeeming nature, we have renewed hope. This section illustrates *God*'s infinite love by exposing *His* generous mercy and grace, freeing us all from condemnation and our personal prisons.

Grace for the Broken
Who Am I?
Mere Words
Just a Walk
How Much Do You Love Me?
The Well
Bruised and Battered – All for a Purpose
There is No Other
More than a Man

GRACE FOR THE BROKEN

*W*hat will I notice? Who will I see? What will catch my attention if I look beyond the reflection of me? Will I see the hurting, those trapped within their past? Will I notice the lost? Those who are down and can't find their way back? Certainly, they are all around us, walking along their lonely trampled paths. They don't seem any different, but they are indeed broken. Of this I have no doubt.

Take just a moment. Pause to look about. Search deeper than the surface, and you will hear their hearts beating, crying out. For theirs is a story, written and told several times before. It's a tale of discovery, where despair does unfold. And now they stumble ahead painfully, moving from to thru fro. On the inside they feel desperate, yet outside, they are afraid to say that so. They pretend they are complete, and they try hard to make that what is known. But broken they are still, and sadly far, far from whole.

They live an existence spent hiding to avoid the light. Fearful its illumination will expose their misguided flight. Surviving in the shadows, they walk a thin, fine line.

Seeking after life's illusion, but instead what's become harder to find – is a peace to accompany, one which will release their captive mind. And so they continue onward, traveling down that same worn road. Without ever realizing they are more broken, the farther along they go.

From a distance, I watch them with intrigue. With a glance, I take pity. To myself aloud I ponder, "What must they have been thinking?" For if life's justice is the consequence of your own wrongdoing, then to the broken I am convinced, they merely got what they had coming!

But in that same instance, practically during that same utterance. In a matter of mere seconds, awakened am I by *Your* bold statements...

> *"Don't act so arrogantly! Don't condemn so quickly! For you too are broken, it's just differently. Your edges now of which are smoothed, were once roughly defined. Your life now may be in order, but thanks be only to The Great Divine. You too would still be hopeless. You too would be dead and alone. You too would still be helpless, if not for my grace, overflowing from my throne."*

WHO AM I?

*W*ho am I, does anyone know? Of what significance do I hold? Of what worth do I bestow? I am a simple man, made simply of skin and bone. I am not a giant; not invincible. My weakness is clear, painfully defined. My strength a mirage, at times impossible to find. My beauty it lingers, if only for a while. But my frailty endures, steadfast beyond trial. My days are spent wondering, worrying 'what if?' And when night comes, I toil under a growing uncertainty within. I chase answers to questions, and then question the reply. Oh *God*, where am I going? When will I get there? And most importantly who am I?

Daily I walk a line, dim as it is thin. Frequently I trip over it, in my confusion only to get back up again. I rise where I've fallen, standing tall yet cowering inside. Fear has its grip on me – I'm terrified to be alive. I walk in a world where boundaries are obscured. I chase after lies where truth is blurred. I strive to stay upright, but regret knocks me down. It is a fierce wind that blows, with shame its one condemning sound. Relentless as it is hopeless, tirelessly it reminds. I'm held captive by the mistakes I've made, imprisoned by the failings I thought I'd left behind. My identity I challenge. The face in the mirror I do not recognize. "Who are you," I ask this reflection and "Pray tell, just who am I?"

Sadly, the image has no response. His expression as puzzled as mine. We look at each other intently, but neither can rightly describe. We have had no revelation. We've received no inspiration. Instead, we stare blankly, and silence amplifies our desperation. While anxiety creeps inward, frustration crawls outward. Will clarity ever reveal itself? Does anyone know who I am? Anyone – anyone at all?

In truth's absence, I am forced to wait. In truth's absence, I'm left to simply contemplate. Careful to consider who it is I've been, those decisions I've made, and to what exactly was their end. And in so doing, truth I do find, but not of the kind I can proudly boast or boldly justify. For more than once I've failed to do what was right, I've stolen, I've cursed, and frankly I've lied. I've envied, I've taken for granted. Sadly, I've ignored the empty-handed. I've cheated, I've hurt. I've even left the helpless alone, stranded. Frequently I allow my desires to become my self-serving guide. Befriended by a conscience, who, without objection agreeably stepped to the side. Disappointingly this is the real me. The man in the mirror all along I've seen. His are the actions that I wish I did not have to believe. But his are the actions I must, for it was him, unquestionably. Oh, what purpose did I serve? Whoa, what punishment do I deserve! I raise my fist high to the sky, and in disgust, aloud I cry, "*WHO... AM... I!*"

And quietly I hear, through raindrops sprinkled in tears:

"You are my creation. You have intention here. I have chosen you; you did not find me. I have designs for your

life that you cannot foresee. Rest in my love, for I am The
God above. Your battle is over. The victory is The Lord's!
— Take courage in this promise; take hope in this procla-
mation! Death has been defeated. All glory belongs to the
risen Son!"

At such kindness, I shudder. At such grace, I shake. At such generosity though I pause, I can't help but hesitate. After all I've said, after all I've done. Who am I to be granted a pardon? Who am I but an onerous one?

And *Your* words they continue where mine rendered short,

"My child your ransom was paid only to spare this father
a broken-heart. Nothing could you do would ever gain my
favor. This is my eternal gift to you, at the cost of a
rugged cross, its brutal nails, and their humble Savior.
Yes, your life has had its hardships. And stumble you
surely did. Still my mercy is far greater, your transgres-
sions I forgive. I did not create you for demise, instead a
future bright. So, take my yoke upon your shoulders. Its
burden is easy and it is light. For mighty are my hands,
and redeeming is my plan. I've always known what I was
doing. My precious child, this is Who I Am!"

MERE WORDS

*M*ere words will not do *You* justice, but mere words are all that I have. They fail to capture the depth of my gratitude or the vastness of my sincerity. Then again, what on earth is capable of this daunting task? Words are not bought or sold; cannot be weighed or measured. Surely, they will not be stored in a chest of treasure. In fact, they are worthless to this world. Mere words are far from fit to honor a *Righteous King* but what alternatives do I have? *You* hold the riches of the universe within the very palm of *Your* hand, and sadly, my hands are those of a beggar, empty, stained by dirt, sweat and sin. My troubled heart is deeply seared as it wrestles with the lingering question, "To *The One* whom I owe everything, what of real value do I have to give?"

Careful reflection of my life draws me to an unavoidable conclusion. Nothing I possess is worthy of *You* or *Your* splendor except my words – true to their meaning and delivered directly from the soul. They are the sacred stones; the precious jewels of my consciousness thought. And I bring them delicately before *You*, placing them on *Your* hallowed alter. May my words be beautiful and glorious, and loyal to their mission of showering *You* with the upmost of praise and grandeur. I pray they rain down eloquently upon *You*, covering *Your* perfect face justly with tribute and glory. May my words reach far into the heavens and shout *Your* name above all names. *You* are *King* of kings, *Lord* of lords, and *You* stand alone at the throne of holy. *You* are so great, so wonderful, so amazing, and so honorable.

My thoughts tremble hesitantly at the very idea of describing *Your* exquisiteness. Everything *You* touch is a masterful design – an artistic wonderment. How can I, a simple man, simply living, wholly depict the holiness that is *Your* pure and virtuous essence? *You* are beauty and majesty, brilliance and radiance, mercy and grace all wrapped into one. *You* are infinite and finite, the lion and the lamb. *The Creator of the Universe* who dwells within the confines of my fragile heart. *You* are ultimate love and ultimate hope – a breath of life in a lifeless tomb. *You* willingly offer eternity to any who ask, and the only question that really needs asked is, "How can *You* be so gracious?"

Who am I to have such honor? *You* call me *Your* child, and I cling hungrily to the sound? What have I done to deserve such kindness? Each and every day I stumble from transgression to transgression, and yet, *You* forgive regardless. I cannot help but fall to my knees at the idea of *Your* compassion. Daily I am besieged by the same profound awakening – *You*, the embodiment of all power and strength, boldly walked towards the cross so I, a feeble self-serving man, could desperately run from it. For this, I am ever grateful. A more beautiful friendship would be unimaginable. A more sanctified union would be unattainable. A more precious gift could I never ask for. And a more deserved fate should I have faced. I am indebted to *You* for so much more than is humanly possible to bestow. All I can do is just whisper "Thank You!" Nothing is more appropriate, and nothing is more complete. I thank you sincerely for allowing me to come before *You*. I thank you sincerely for listening. And I thank you sincerely for saving me from myself and my impending sentence of death.

I am overcome with gratitude. Mighty are *You* and lowly am I. There is no reason for *You* to show concern for me. *You* have long existed without me and would continue to forever. However, my life is hopeless and impossible without *Your* presence. I am intertwined within *Your* bosom. In the midst of all *Your* magnificence, *You* never abandon or forsake me. *You* always watch over me, helping me even when I am unaware *You* are there. *You* are so benevolent, so caring, and so considerate. *You* treat me as I am the treasure *You* search to find. How can this be, I am only a man? Despite my chaotic existence, *You* grant me unquestionable serenity. *You* supply me with such peace and such provision. I take rest in *Your* arms and tranquility in the faith which *You* sustain.

To an *Almighty God*, who makes all things possible, I owe *You* my life. I was a ship lost at sea, but *You* are a trustworthy captain who rescued me, redeeming me. My entire being now has truly one yearning: for *Your* name to be exalted above all others.

I know my words are humble, plain, and ordinary, but they express the heartfelt longing of man who desires to worship *You* and *You* alone. With love in my heart and my heart in mind, I have knit the most lovely and cherished of them together into a majestic tapestry. Please, waive it high in the sky as a banner of conquest. Take these words and consider them my lamb of sacrifice. Know that I write to commend *You*. I write to admire *You*. And most importantly, I write to love *You*. It is honest and absolute and epitomizes my core belief. This is a promise, a pledge, a proclamation – my eternal offering. And rest assured, it is certainly not mere words.

JUST A WALK

They coaxed him from the crib and onto the floor. A parent's proudest moment was soon to be in store. This was a rite of passage; an act passed throughout time. Everyone must take it. Everyone must cross that line. So as he climbed to his feeble and trembling feet, his tiny legs steadied him, calming his heart's now quickened beat. This was not their first time attempting this feat, but hopefully it would be the last of him falling back to his seat. Anxious onlookers watched intently, ready to catch. But confidence exuded. His foe gravity today had met its match. There's a world that beckons – for him it awaits. But first, he must cross the threshold and open its gate. With his parents to witness, triumph was mere seconds away. "It's just a walk," they said, their ambitious visions racing on this memorable day.

And his next twenty years seemed to speed right by. As this boy grew, his future looked clear and it looked bright. His aspirations were high, and his agenda defined. His mission was noble, and his timing was ripe. He was now set to step into the real world, about to take his flight. He had a number of dreams and an idealistic cause to fight. As he turned the tassel and straightened the gown, again his parents were eagerly looking down. Neither had ever been there before, and so they were unsure of precisely what to bestow. "It's just a walk," they said, relying on words of old. These pearls of wisdom they thought every man should know, seemed to describe best the journey on which he was engaged to go.

All was moving smoothly as he began his new life. And for several years to follow, he managed to avoid any significant strife. But a few bad choices here and a couple of compromises there, left him at a crossroads he would later regret to bear. The trust in a friend and lack of good judgment as well sent his life spiraling, yet sadly, no one could tell. His thirst for success and prosperity to share, was blinding and deceiving, overshadowing the risk and the desire to care. To him who started so honest and pure, he suddenly found himself in a predicament of which he couldn't draw clear. Down a track far from where he ever intended to stay, clumsily he and his comrades stumbled and slowly slipped astray. "It's just a walk," they said, together as they followed that crooked path. Justifying their behavior at the expense of their gaffe.

It wasn't long after when finally he broke. The existence he had chosen was neither a blessing, nor offered any hope. Integrity and character, two qualities he cherished the most, had become just words to be taken halfheartedly – something some might consider a joke. Their absence in his heart left a hole too big to fill. So upon bended knees he cried out, to the *God* he believed in still. And like a phoenix arises from the ash where it lays. A second chance was reborn, a new road was divinely paved. His essence again had meaning, but not of the worldly kind. Frankly though it didn't matter because assurance was in his *Savior* who had bridged the great divide. In addition, those closest to him never abandoned his shaken side, thankfully allowing him forgiveness and a renewed chance to thrive. Their expression to him was the same as he had heard before each time a pivotal moment was knocking on his door. Sincerely and kindly, they spoke of his alternative route instead, gracefully and honorably disregarding his failings, "It's just a walk," they said.

His remaining days flew by like a flash. Soon it was his turn to cross into the next realm; to sprint that final, unknown, unseen dash. And as he did, he couldn't help but to fret and to fear. For what exactly would he see and what exactly would he hear? While he wandered deep into *Death's Shadowy Valley*, he looked all around, this was truly the first time he'd been alone, and he was solemnly worried. Afraid and uncertain he was now fully aware. All he wanted was comfort, but from whom and from where? So, in order to find for that which he longed he reflected back on a thought from before he'd passed-on. "It's just a walk," he said, trying desperately to calm his frightened soul, and bring peace to his mind which had forgotten the eternal goal.

But to his great surprise, brilliance filled his eyes. From seemingly out of nowhere, he was joined by the *Saving One – The Messiah*, descending from the sky. A host of others then crowded around. Mere words could not describe the joyous newfound sound. Down came their triumphant cheers, rolling like thunder. Surrounding him ever prouder, ever louder, growing ever stronger. The roar of the saints who'd gone before, was certainly deafening; it could not be ignored. They chanted, "Glory to *God*, for another one has escaped death's dreaded awe. And victory was again claimed from the Dragon's tyrannical claw! And although this man's journey was never easy, and occasionally he did fall, he never gave up, and our *God*, *The Redeemer*, remained faithful through it all!" The man so overjoyed he could hardly speak. To the *Lord* he just turned and sighed with relief. And from the lips of true *Father* and a true friend, came the words he will forever cherish, "My child say goodbye to your sin, this love story is only beginning and not at its end!" And with that the two ascended toward *Heaven* and the spectacular splendor within. But awestruck the man paused before going on in. Sensing his hesitation, *Jesus* stopped and turned directly to him. "It's just a walk," *Jesus* said, as *His* smile turned into a loving, radiant grin!

HOW MUCH DO YOU LOVE ME?

*S*ince the dawn of time, many questions have been pondered – questions as countless as the stars. Everyone has something which captures their wonderment, however for me, one query rises to the top. "Just how much do *You* love me?"

I have often thought this thought. I contemplate about much, yet this ambiguity seems to surface more than most. I hear others speak of *Your* love, but do they truly understand? It is said that *You* love all, but to what degree do *You* cherish me?

Just how much do *You* love me? I wrestle with this unknown notion. It intrigues my intellect. It stirs my soul to simmer. It challenges my curiosity and causes my imagination to implode. Such a question, with no apparent way of knowing, and no one to ask directly. Will my inquiry ever be satisfied?

Quietly, I wait for a response, and quietly, *You* do respond...

*"My precious child you'll never truly comprehend
    my love."*
My curiosity chiding me, I contest, "Can you
    measure it with a number?"
You reply simply, *"Surely, that would be
    infinity!"*
Sensing cynicism, I scoff, but *You* gently state,
    "Its sincerity, you mistook".
Not content, I counter, "I am desperate to
    know, please just describe a little and I
    will resign the thought."
Silence is *Your* return.
My frustration swells! How can *You* be so
    insufferable and leave me feeling so
    isolated and alone?

Then my mind's eye reflects back to a day on Calvary – the chaos, the cross, the crimson collage. It is clear who suffered, hanging alone. The conclusion to my inquest has been there all along. The once stained soil I now stand to engage *You* on has been washed clean. My emotions and my insecurities left me hungry, desperate for a shout from the heavens. Instead, I got a whisper in the wind. My fears formerly entangled my reason. Now my reason untangles my fears. One question has echoed throughout the ages and one answer will resound through eternity – *"Your* blood says it all!"

> *The blood of the lamb and the breath of a lion.*
>   *How awesome are You!*
> *You are so full of love and so willing to share.*
>   *How abounding are Your hands!*

*You have the face of the sun with the purity of the
moon. How astonishing is Your presence!
In You, lies the wisdom of the ages with the
ambition of youth. How abiding is Your reign!*

How much do *You* love me is often the inquisition, but
how much can I love *You* is the real wonder.

THE WELL

*D*aily I walk, and daily I thirst, yet my body knows no difference. I have always existed in such a state as this and so, I continue on, unaware of my deficiency, oblivious to any need. My body is slow to deplete, but rest assured, slowly, it is depleting. It isn't until I hit the rock of bottom that I realize something is lacking and I have run dry.

Once detecting my distress, I am frantic to find a fix – something, which will meet my missing means. I immediately look for a quick quench, a reprieve from my parchedness. I search everywhere from high to low, from worldly wisdom to fame and fortune. Nothing I find lasts long enough to leave me sustained. Each provides an initial relief, and then quickly, quietly fades into the darkness and I am left more desperate than before – more emptied than I thought I could be. I dread my body and soul are somberly running out of time.

Where can I go to fill my cup? Where can I find water that will relieve my thirst? I know of no such well deep enough to keep me from thirsting again. They too run their course over time. Eventually they will evaporate and be no more. They must! It is impossible not to, right?

My unyielding search leads me nowhere but to my knees in despair. Out into the sky I cry and from above, I hear the questions,

> "Where have you looked to fill your cup? Where have you turned to find your peace? I have been here all along; from before time began, to the time it will end. My throne will last forever. Do you not know you are my child, my creation of love? I offer you my riches as an inheritance. If you are thirsty, take your cup to my well – the well of Jacob and Abraham, of David and Israel, and of you of course, all my children. Once sipping you will never thirst again. This is my promise to you, my sacred vow. Never to be changed, never to be challenged, and only to be honored for an eternity. You need do nothing more than ask; you need do nothing less than seek. I will be here waiting and, if you are willing than just drink and see what I am offering."

Such an offer I cannot refuse. Such an invitation I cannot ignore! For whatever reason I am loved, and for whatever reason I am sought. And so, I will accept this gift, I will accept my inheritance and drink.

Once I taste, an overwhelming peace settles in. My mind is calm, and I am aware. My body and spirit are fulfilled and most importantly, my cup runs over. My heart is full and my soul content.

To *The Well* will I now come; to *The Well* will I forever cling. Who am I to want? *You* grant me peace and *You* grant me hope! Who am I to long? Oh, how I wish to one day see *Your* face. Oh, how I dream to one day stand at *Your* gate. There, I know it will all make sense – a life of sacrifice and rejection to be rewarded by an eternity of bliss. Oh, to live forever! Oh, to the glory! And all because of one small sip.

BRUISED AND BATTERED

ALL FOR A PURPOSE

My *God*, *You* are *The Savior*
who's pierced side did flow,
Both water and blood
that pooled on the ground below.

Sin's stain quickly reddening the dirt turned mud,
All the while, redemption soaring high overhead,
on the wings of a snow-white dove.

Poured out *Your* life in an unending adoration,
Selfless, *You* who were wounded for and by
Your beloved, clay creation.
Once called beautiful and righteous,
now cursed at as an abhorrent,
ugly abomination.

Onlookers not noticing,
but believing the battle ultimately lost,
You hung, tirelessly on that criminal's
unforgiving, rugged, wooden cross.

But with victory tenuously wrapped
between the jaws of defeat,
You never did waiver, surrender, or think to retreat!
Persevering through *Your* very last heartbeat!

"It is finished!" *You* pronounced,
breathing *Your* last,
This sacrifice now fulfilled
from the lot so long ago cast.

Sanctification masked as an "execution of damnation,"
Though it disguised a crime,
truly a plan of glorious salvation!

This plight not just a hollow, empty promise,
Rather a ransom with an eternal,
Heavenly, planned purpose.

The price, a purchase much too steep for
any one to afford,
Yet *You* paid it all because
You are the holy, redeeming, risen *Lord*!

A binding proclamation made all those years ago,
"Mankind is loved and forever restored!
"To the sinner and saint alike,
everywhere let it now be known,
"Sorrow has no grip
on those who trust
in the *Almighty Redeemer of Souls!*"

THERE IS NO OTHER

The road of every man is marked with eager anticipation and great expectation. He is bold and proud, and enthusiastically encounters life. Often alone but rarely afraid, he approaches his days as a self-fulfilling prophesy – reaching as far as he can, taking ahold of anything he can grasp. He looks to the stars and calls out his very name. Hoping to leave a legacy that reigns down from the heavens above. He is undivided and unbound; unique, unveiled, and unrivaled. He is special. There is no other.

Who he can be is limitless, who he is is temporary. He strives to be the one he is destined to become. As obstacles roll his way, he needs only to have courage and conviction to hurdle them in stride. And so, he leaps, not to be dissuaded by the landing. Sometimes he sails; other times, he sprawls. Either way, his determination is unyielding because he has plotted clearly his own route. Success is his only battle cry. There is no other.

As he navigates his life, he hears others speak of hardship – how time is fleeting and stamina failing. But he is different. Youth is his ally and strength is his companion. He considers his confidence a blessing, but ironically, his arrogance has blinded him. And in the midst of his momentum, his missteps have mounted. A course previously mapped start to finish, has reached an impasse, and he is now encircled within a conundrum. His journey has reached its apparent end. Shock and confusion overwhelm his emotion. How can this be, there is no other?

He looks to the same sky and asks it for an answer. Not sure what he'll hear, he waits for its reply. As the earth turns and the cosmos stir, it becomes clear. His dependence upon himself to sustain was mistakenly deprived of an eternal flame. What he thought was his destiny to obtain, is lacking divine design. He is forced into inner reflection and outer acknowledgement. And so, desperate, upon bended knees he finds himself bracing – a position of true submission. There is no other.

And true to the very nature of the *God of the Universe*, he is not left forsaken. A past ransom has again rescued a future generation. He is reminded that a wooden cross, bearing a beaten man, which bore an empty grave and an eternity of grace, is redeemable to any who would ask. And he, who once believed needed only himself, is humbled at that thought. Like all, he was hopeless and lost. But, by the grace of *God* alone, a path formerly impossible to pass is provided a passage through a bridge resurrected! There is no other!

> *"There Is Only One God... One Savior...*
> *One Hope... One Life... One Way...*
> *There Is No Other!"*

MORE THAN A MAN

I am nothing more than a man; here today, gone tomorrow. Similar to other men, I too am oblivious to how vulnerable I truly am. My frailty is overshadowed by my own shadow. My humanity loses its humility to my vanity. My nature is self-seeking, self-centered and self-promoting. My motives are not to be trusted. Sometimes they are pure, but most of the others, posturing. They deceive me and declare me guilty of treason to the *Most High*. In addition, transgression tempts me, and I balance daily between crossing the line and toeing it. What's more, I wrestle with a flimsy faith – battling to resist doubt and reject confusion. Their constant attacks are something I can count on as sure as the sun rises. Some days I win; others I don't. I fear I will never be fully free from their barrage and able to focus on the moments with faithfulness, void of volatility and weakness. It's painfully clear that when I take account of myself, I am aware that I am nothing more than a man – wretched and weak!

Like all men, my hands are an essential part of who I am. They are my tools; they are my trade. Without them, I would suffer to survive. Without them, I would be helpless. They were created to assist and affect my life in a manner for which I can depend on them without fail. Alongside of me they grow. They are my best friends, my most trusted companions. They should never falter. Uniquely they depict my life's story. Their lines, their calluses, detail my strife, my scars, my sorrows. Sadly, though, they are disloyal, and provide disservice in the face of decision. They grasp for the things of this world – the things I desire – the things I tell them are most important for success and praise, rather than reaching out, open, and apologetic, stretching for the things that will spare my soul and save myself from myself. Deceptively, they work against me, disarming my heart by their selfish desires and their sinful strategies. My hands are a necessary part of me, but they don't necessarily perform accordingly. They are not noble. They are those of an ordinary man's – nothing more, and repeatedly they betray the glorious purpose for which they were designed.

Not to be outdone, a man is not complete without his feet. They are his means of transportation and his determinant of fruitfulness. From the moment he learns to rely on them, they act uniformly, carrying him through consciousness, advancing him on the road toward achievement. They serve to help him travel the world and traverse the journey of life. Whether large or small, they are of great importance. Unfortunately though, like other men, my feet, are those of a forgetful son's – walking in unison away from the light and forging ahead into the unknown of night. They are unaware of the impending dangers that loom. Unaffected by the past predicaments of peril that wane. But still they proceed, nonetheless. They continue their march, oblivious to my eventual demise. Their goal is simple: to save their soles. However, they do not act alone. They do what they are told, proclaiming my independence instead of my dependence on the *Creator of the Universe*. Their mission is to meet my needs and nobody else's. Despite their potential, they yield to their host – a man, who is nothing more than that which he races after, eternal emptiness. And although, initially they produced my first steps toward freedom, ironically in so doing, they also rendered my last towards innocence.

At the heart of it, is perhaps the most significant piece of me, my heart. It is the source of my existence. My heart is essential for physical stability, but also emotional sustainability. It provides the lifeblood I need to live, and it stores the hopes I need to dream. Without it, all of me would die. While it is not just situated in the center of my chest, it does lie at the core of my very being. It contains my character, which determines my direction by deciphering my intentions. My heart is responsible for my reasoning, and it drives my decisions. Unmistakably, the prospect for a healthy, happy life flows directly through my heart. However, it too abandons its calling. Its capacity to lead a man is uncanny, and all too often, it leads me astray. Even though, at times I may have the best of intentions, I am routinely plagued by the worst of ambitions, and I fall victim to compromise and cowardliness. Despite the potential for promise, usually my selfish agenda is all it pursues. Continually I am reminded, I am just a man, nothing more. And although in every man is the breath of his *Maker*, within me, I make very little room for *Him* inside my most treasured part – my heart.

For all these reasons, I am in dire need of a *Savior*. Someone to operate independently of me to secure my future. I cannot save myself. In fact, I work desperately to destroy myself. My single interest is in promoting my importance. I could never stand alone, for I would eventually be devoured. My shame is in my weakness; my shame is in my pride. Who am I but a man, nothing more. And similar to other men, ego entices me to resist the help I need. It prevents me from asking for direction from *The Devine*.

Thankfully, though, in spite of my efforts to ignore *You*, *Your Will* would not allow *You* to forget me. *You* provided a way to restore right standing for all of those *You* cherish, including me. The plan – *Your* plan – needed a lamb, so *You* became man, a commitment unprecedented and unparalleled. *You* laid *Your* life down as a sacrifice to prove *Your* devotion and what a man was truly capable of. *Your* faithfulness cannot be matched. *Your* hands, *Your* feet, *Your* heart each boldly pronounce *Your* love. In contrast to mine, *Your* hands grasp for that which is righteous, even though they were pierced. *Your* feet search for the lost and needy, even though they were torn. *Your* heart loves all as well as those who despise *You*, even though it was broken. There is none like *You*. *You* spare man in spite of his ignorant arrogance, and *Your* grace and mercy sustain him and me every day. Time and time again, I prove I am nothing more than a man. But *You*, *You* were definitely more than just a man, and day-in and day-out *You* prove *You* are nothing less than a loving *Father*, magnificent *Creator*, and *The One True God*!

3

PEACE AND HOPE

*P*eace and Hope concentrates on rendering clarity to a cloudy perception. Life can become over-whelming, and unless you have an endless well with an eternal spring of love, you will always be wanting. These pieces return the focus to *God*, the place where it rightly belongs, thus allowing us to see the stars while we are navi-gating the seas.

Today God Stopped By
There's Strength in You
He Thinks I Can
A Light Pierces the Darkness
Alone
The New Day
And Yet the Sun Rises
Little Flock
Hopeless

TODAY GOD STOPPED BY...

*T*oday *God* stopped by and it wasn't expected! *He* surprised me; I didn't see *Him* coming. *He* caught my attention, like the reflection of a mirror. No, it didn't come from the corner of my eye, nor did *He* startle me into submission. *He* didn't stand up and shout or sneak *His* way in through an open window. *He* just kind of smiled, and I felt *His* warm presence. *He* offered me that peace of mind that I couldn't substitute as someone else's. Strangely, I knew *He* was near – *He* left such an unmistakable impression. Yes, today *God* stopped by, and *He* didn't even have a reservation!

Today *God* stopped by, though at first, I didn't quite recognize *Him*. *He* wasn't where I anticipated and truthfully, I wasn't truly looking. I was deep in thought, busy wrestling with my feelings. Wondering what to do next; wondering what would happen next; just plain wondering. When all of a sudden there *He* was, centered amongst the distractions. Rearranging my moments into a moment, one worth remembering. *His* hands were gentle, as they softly squeezed my shoulders. And *His* voice was calm, reassuring me I was treasured. Yes, today *God* stopped by, and it helped to lift my spirits!

Today *God* stopped by, but when *He* began to speak, I must confess I wasn't really listening. In fact, it took me just a second to realize who was even talking. *His* tone sounded familiar, coming from out of nowhere. Yet *His* words were undeniable, breaking-in through the silence. *His* questions were engaging, at times even poignant. And *His* intentions became clearer, evident with every question. *He* was simply checking on me – seeing how I was doing. Uncovering my emotions, those I'd kept hidden. *He* was interested in specifics, to *Him* they each had purpose. *He* was taking *His* time to remind me I was someone *He* found very special. Yes, today *God* stopped by just to share with me a visit.

Today *God* stopped by while I was all wrapped-up in my contemplation. "How are you?" *He* politely asked, "And about what are you thinking?" *He* wasn't prodding or trying to be intimidating. *He* was just curious, and to me this was comforting. For lately I'd become frustrated, comparing myself to others. Aware that when it came to trophies and ribbons, disappointedly I had neither. "Am I doing enough?" I replied, sincerely responding to *His* inquiry. "Am I who *You* want me to be, and where on Earth do *YOU* need me?" These were my thoughts if I am being upfront and honest. But *God* who knows all, was very direct, challenging my mind's conventional understanding. *"I've called you to be you!" He* said, *"That's why I made you." "Your purpose is to serve only where it is that I have led you."* And with that, our conversation ended, but not without me reaching its profound conclusion! For who was I to argue with the hands of my wise *Creator*? Yes, today *God* stopped by adding clarity to my shortsighted vision.

Today *God* stopped by, but it was only for a minute. *He*

didn't stay too long – *His* time there was fleeting. Still, in those seconds what I found will last longer than a lifetime. For *His* words made their impact, depositing in me the very thing I needed. And as we parted, I realized this encounter went way beyond coincidental. Because it's not every day *The King of Universe* shows-up; now I too have a monument to place atop my heart's mantle! Yes, today *God* stopped by and I couldn't help but pause to take notice!

And I said, "What about him Lord?" Jesus answered, "...You, me, follow." John 21: 21-22

THERE'S STRENGTH IN YOU...

*T*here's strength in you; something so beautiful and true. It shines like the sun, radiating through and through. It's reflected in the words you say and captured by the things you do. It's the heart of your being – the very color of your bloom. Strength alone does not define you but the times it crosses my mind are more than a few. For when I think of the hardships you have faced, perseverance reveals it powerfully renewed.

There's strength in you; I see it clearly each day. It's visible from up-close, and still noticeable from far away. It's like a picture that never ages, fading from black to grey. Nor does it blur around its edges, blending distinction into a multicolored array. It's a quality rarely seen. Yet in you, amplified on display. And perhaps it's at its finest, the moments when silence is all we have to say. As quietly you stand alongside, encouraging my every which way – offering a firm shoulder to lean-on, and a gentle confidante to hear me pray.

There's strength in you; of this I have no doubt. In fact, it's the one characteristic that mirrors truly what you really are all about! Where with others I worry, would flee at the first sound of a battle shout. In you there is no faltering. You're a comrade I could never do without. Your presence provides peace, and your essence never proud. What a special friend I have in you, a treasure too valuable to ever count!

There's strength in you; so much I fail to rightly mention. It was placed there by *God* above, as part of *His* gloriously designed, purposeful intention. While you may not always feel it, believe in spite of any reservation. It will not disappear. It's eternally supplied from *The One* who is *Holy and Perfection*! And upon *Him*, do we cast all hope with no hesitation. For nothing is impossible to the *Lord God Almighty*, that 'Strength' we see in your radiant reflection!

HE THINKS I CAN

*I*t doesn't matter what I think because *He* thinks I can. My mind will lead me astray; my mind will convince me to wander into the realm of doubt, wondering in disbelief. My mind will trick and deceive. It lies silent, cowardly in-wait for weakness to tell me I cannot. My mind calls me a fool, but it doesn't matter what my mind thinks because *He* thinks I can!

Others laugh when I speak of '*My Calling*'. They remind me of my imperfections, counting aloud my missteps – tallying for the crowd my mistakes. They call to attention my several flaws, pointing out my many falls. Do they not believe I have been given a new name and a divine direction? They curse the idea of my destination-minded approach, trying to persuade me to live in desperation without hope. They question my purpose, but they don't hear the words of *My Maker*. It doesn't' matter what others think because *He* thinks I can!

The world says I'm going the wrong way. It yells for me to stop and turn back before I get lost. "Lost" is its biggest fear, but I know I'm never lost since *You* have led me to this place. Lost is the helpless cry of the lonely. It is not the promise of *The Lord*. On *Lost's* shores, banks the reservoir of the dead. While on the beaches of *The Found*, lies the source, the living life-spring reserved for the followers of *Christ*. In its spite, *Lost* seeks to drown others as to not dwell alone. Yet from *The Found*, surfaces a glorious revival where the sinner recognizes he is not saved on his own. The world will reject the righteous, but it doesn't matter what the world thinks because *He* thinks I can!

This road I'm on is my journey – it's not simply a means to my end. This road has bumps and misdirection, twists and turns. Thankfully though it also has clear signs and straight lines. It's not the road paved for you. It's the road *He* shaped for me. Indeed, this road is not mapped, nor can I see where it always leads or when it ends. This road's story may be untold, still it doesn't matter if the course is not known because *He* thinks I can!

I will fail; I will triumph. I will stumble; I will hurdle. I will crawl; I will stand tall. My faith is not in me, but in *He*, who is in control of it all. I don't' have to know where I'm going; I just need to trust *He* does. *He* is *Truth*; *He* is *Light*; *He* is a lamp unto my feet. *He* doesn't just help when I pray, *He* helps when I don't. *He's* the *God Who* Is, and *He* thinks I can!

A LIGHT PIERCES THE DARKNESS

*W*hen darkness surrounds, direction can be hard to find. For where does a man turn in a world that is round? If he looks to his left or glances back right, neither will reveal the path for him to take outright. In the end he is walking in a circle, blinded by absence. Not really here nor there, he is truly far from anywhere. He is a traveler traveling that can't see the road below. And then a light pierces the darkness...

Awakened by profound understanding, how long have I been asleep? Who has been speaking into my life and where have these steps taken me? I wonder at that. When did I become so lost and why couldn't I recognize my waywardness? I'm almost too afraid to ask. It seems only dim depictions have grown where the shadows did cast. But there has to be more than what I had been shown. There is purpose to my being, deep down I feel it so. I just need a spark – something real I can grasp. And then a light pierces the darkness...

A hand from above reaches down to pull me close. A whisper in the wind calls, declaring my worth. Me significant? How can that be? I was just one among many, what makes me cherished from any of these? And like the phoenix who arises from ash, I'm revived with newfound hope. My mind implores at things I'd never thought before. Once I was a prisoner, trapped and destined to die. Now I am forgiven, set free, and fully alive. What grace has extended mercy has accepted. And then a light pierces the darkness...

My eyes no longer veiled I can see. My heart no longer bound-up in lies, I am released. I am consciously aware – to worship *The Creator* is to know *Thy Maker*. *He* is *The Lord God Almighty*, who always reigns. *His* is the way, the truth, and the life, from eternity past forevermore. Never to be undone or will *He* lose that which *He* holds. *He* is the one who calls me by name, watching over my days in complete. In *His* greatness, *God* made a way through the wilderness, and I am eternally saved. And then a light pierces the darkness...

> *Sin ran away with the soul, but God, in His love, sent a Savior to rescue the young – to recover the old. Man needed a redeemer, and he received his Lord. A baby born to a world torn. Angels sang about it, and shepherds proclaimed it so. "Immanuel has come! The King of the Universe does call a manger for His throne." Mercy, forgiveness, and hope delivered straight from Heaven's door. None who asks will ever be ignored, and ALL who seek, will be faithfully and fully restored. The Light has forever pierced the darkness!*

ALONE

*H*ow do I dream of tomorrow when I am terrified I won't escape today? This question is haunting, holding me captive, as I stare wearily out my eyes into the darkness. I am awaiting the arrival of dawn, but for me, a new morning does not bring a new hope. My brain becomes flooded with an onslaught of emotions as it is over-taken in the same way the sun lays siege to the night, roaring past the dimly lit horizon into an unmarked sky. I feel helplessly trapped within myself – unsure of how to tackle the complexities of this day while wrestling with the failings of yesterday and yesteryear. Panic leaps into my chest, suffocating my tired and tattered heart. I turn to flee but have nowhere to turn. It is painfully clear there is no running from my life. My very being becomes fully aware, things will not change and I... I am alone.

How do I now engage today, knowing the game I am forced to play grants no winners, only losers? This world I have come to know is callous, unforgiving and uncompro-mising. Despite all of my best efforts, my past labors have left me trailing. Inside my mind I see my life as it should be, beautifully intertwined with dreams and hopes come true. I am accomplishing all I have set out to do and, furthermore, doing it in a way in which my wake leaves harmony and prosperity to those around. Although my ambitions are noble and sincere, tragically, they do not materialize. They are left discouraged by reality and its harsh truth – she is bitter, cold, and leaves only an insatiable thirst – unyielding, unrelenting, and at times unbearable. I cannot help feeling weak and broken as my core cries out, longing to know when will things change, if ever. I strive to cling to my desires but even they fall victim, slipping from my grasp. And I once again am mindful, I am alone.

Desperate, I seek help from others who might be able to pull me from the claws of the looming hours. I am wishful they will shed some glimmer of insight into my painful and impossibly hopeless journey. They however, struggle to understand my fight. Frustratingly, they want to point to a big, beautiful, grand, and glorious picture of life, attempting to convince me to overlook the individual moments in search of the broader brushed portrait. They do not realize ignoring the single droplets of paint, seemingly scattered recklessly upon the canvas, is perilous to someone who is just trying simply to weather today's stormy seconds – hesitantly staggering from one to the next. I am not concerned even slightly with what tomorrow brings, for I may not last this very minute. I wish it were not so but undoubtedly they do not recognize the frightening battle in which I am entrenched; and sadly, I am still very, very alone.

As I push forward to make my way through this fruitless day, the weights of my worries force me to the floor. They act uniformly as an intense, backbreaking burden, which I cannot seem to bear. I collect my might and slowly return to my feet; not ready, but willing to face the daunting task of negotiating my daily grind. Although I want nothing more than to quit, something inside forbids surrender. I begin to plod along – one painstaking step in front of another, like a tirelessly aging workhorse not getting anywhere and unable to predict how long he will last. I am unclear of where I am going but going, nonetheless. The sun is cruel and relentless as it beats down heavily. The only thing between me and falling to the ground is the shadow cast in front of me, beside me, and sometimes behind me. How can this be, I ponder, where did it come from, I thought I was alone?

Limping onward, I notice my shadow follows, never leaving but ever changing. It slinks and shrinks, climbs and crawls, as I trudge clumsily across the vast and varying terrain of my walk. Is my shadow the only thing keeping me from collapsing? I question. Surely it must be, for I do not have any capacity of my own. I am exhausted. Mysteriously and suddenly, like a butterfly breaking free from his cocoon and stretching out his wings, from the depths of my hollowed man a metamorphosis of spirit starts to form. My soul is overjoyed beyond comprehension. It is relieved and revived, revisited with a renewed hope that had been hiding but was now pouring out. My thoughts scramble to piece together from where this amazing inner-peace and strength was coming. Why do I now feel like soaring when I was only just barely able to stumble? Quietly though, in the midst of chaos, came calmness and I knew. I remembered a promise to never leave nor forsake me, and this promise was now taking the shape of a shadow – my shadow, serving as a constant companion removing the entangling web of fear claiming I was alone.

Finally, I am calm. I rest. This day has come to a fascinating end, and I am encouraged and enlightened. A vow upheld and honored in the *Most-High* of high places forever changes my life. I can anxiously look to tomorrow since I have now survived today. I am filled with an unending hope in a loving and living *Redeemer*, who is everlasting and fulfills all *His* promises. From this instant through eternity, I will decide to travel in faith, knowing my faith may be hard to find at times, but *He* will not be – all I need do is look down to my shadow. My heart may doubt but I will stand tall and choose to be faithful, cognizant *He* hears my every request. I will relinquish my earthly logic and under-standing of my difficult and trying circumstance, to reach out with open arms – open hands – and closed eyes; boldly proclaiming *He* is *The One* and *Only*. Confidently, I will trust in *The Creator of the Universe* – the *Beacon of Holiness* – the *Author of Love*; and *The Father* of us all. I thank *God* for today because, thanks to today I was reborn, recreated, and reminded I am never alone.

THE NEW DAY

*T*he new day draws near, and my rest comes to an end – just as the shadows of night quietly slip past the rays of the sun's light into the unknown of flight. What does this fresh day have in store? I wonder. Where will my road lead? I ponder. This day is like the others and so I know many are the tasks set before me; many are the pitfalls ready to ensnare me; and many more are the wolves who lie in wait for me. This is a new day but an old one, not unlike the others to come before.

Although these threats are ever present and do not hide, I have never known life to be any different. And so, I do not fear moving forward, but to what my future holds, does cause me to take pause. The uncertainty of living is a captivating, yet petrifying experience both at the same time. Traveling in a world where chaos is engrained within living has become the natural order. But it is still concerning. Will it ever end? Or will it lead to my demise? Thoughts race through my mind and swarm my consciousness like the swelling of the evening tide. I am only a man, and my new day's hopes are snuffed out like the candle's flame.

Because of the constant battle in store – the one I have known from before – I must prepare for whatever may come. I must equip right for my journey outside these walls of security. Victory depends on survival, and survival depends on proper preparation.

The difficulties ahead have waged war, and so now, I am an everyday warrior. In order to defend myself from what's to come I must don the wardrobe of battle. I must wear the helmet and the breastplate, carry the shield and the sword. Their protection is my only hope against whatever lies outside my door – hiding in the shadows. They are the necessary tools I will use to defend my soul and my spirit. Each possesses its own unique charm, and each will be used more than once on this new day. I unpack them tenderly from their carrying case – a cloth covered, tightly bound container of words: a book.

I chase after the world, but the world is not for me. It deceives and misleads, causing me to search frantically in lust. But upon finding what I was looking for, I see emptiness and shallowness. Its treasures are moth ridden and broken, hiding behind a veil of illusion and brokenness. But *You Oh Lord* are what sustains me. *You* are what satisfies my every need. *Your* treasures are not hard to find, and *You* offer them generously. *You* do not disguise them, but rather mark them clearly and provide a guide to help me find them. *Your Will* will direct me to glorious riches the world has never known. They are created for an eternity; all I need do is ask.

The world lies and tricks, sending me down paths that are confusing and entangling. I think I'm going somewhere only to find I have gone nowhere. But *Your* path *Oh Lord* is straight and narrow; clearly defined. *Your* way is perfect and accounts for the unseen. *You* are a lamp unto my feet, and I will follow where *You* lead. For its plain to see, *Your* way is best and I was created to trust *Your* guiding hands. *You* molded me from clay to be *Your* child. *You* shaped my mind and knitted my heart with tenderness and delicacy. *You* have not abandoned me but embraced me. *You* want me to find the world *You* have prepared and not the one it has become.

I am going to search but only for *You*. For it is *You* I wish to find - *You* I wish to know better. My life is meaningless without *You,* and meaningful only when I humbly walk obediently after *You*. With all this in mind, it is easy to see which way I should go, but easier yet to see which way I will go! *Oh Lord, You* are my rock, *You* are my friend through the end!

AND YET THE SUN RISES

For young and old, the night can be scary; it can be terrifying. The shadows secretly move, shifting and shaping around everything and anything they find hiding in the dark. They come crawling from every corner and crevice, expanding into worldly unknowns. The mind wanders to places of uncertainty –places of fret, casting monsters from the creative subconscious. Fear lays siege to the sane. Silent sounds are deafening – unusual and unfamiliar. Children are afraid of what they cannot see, and adults, fear what they can. Sleep does not come quickly, and wide eyes are left straining in the blackness, probing while the tormenting seconds linger. Insecurities are unending and the darkness unyielding. Even though nights come and go, each one seems different from the last; each one posing an uncertain destiny.

And yet the sun rises, and with it, a new dawn. The once dreaded night is washed away gracefully by the warming glow of the sun's light. Each morning it shines – never failing – granting reprieve to the restless. The shadows run cowering back into the places from where they came. Those creations that stirred up fright in the night, now can be seen for what they truly are: figments of an overactive imagination. A renewed sense of peace settles in. A conqueror's spirit resurfaces, rejuvenated at the sight of the first bright ray. With the sweeping might of the sun's light, relief marches boldly into plain sight.

Walking through life too can be dark and scary. Men stumble along, only to encounter obstacle after obstacle – challenge after challenge. They grow weak, they grow weary, tired of battling the pressure and presence of adversity. Man's heart is tested, and thus, tamed. His spirit becomes exhausted as he continually convinces himself to press-on through the long, agonizing storms of living – taunted by the stories of success that opportunity has not afforded him. His frustrations swell, and his feelings of disenchantment intensify. In the midst of chaos, his confusion multiplies and his worry compounds. At times, life's journey appears hopeless and lost, leaving the wanderer to wonder, "What's it all for?" The only thing he knows with certainty is life certainly is not fair.

And yet, *The Son* rises, and with *Him*, a new hope. A glorious eternity is revealed. Lost ambition is returned; a joyful spirit restored. The moments that were so trying before, become trivial, serving as testimonials of the wondrous work of the resurrection. A fresh road is divinely paved, and a new direction is revealed. Justice is finally rendered; evil is damned. What life had forgotten *God* has remembered. Peace is found where pursuit was lost. Although life will continue to impose, the walk will not be in isolation. The traveler is accompanied by *The One* who makes life make sense. As sure as we count on the sun to shine, so too should we rely on *This Son*. Ultimately, darkness cannot hide the truth that through the world, man is reminded of his fragility, but in his *Redeemer*, he is reminded of his fruitful future.

LITTLE FLOCK

*F*ear not little flock, this world is *NOT* falling apart. *The God of the Universe* is still reigning – undeterred and uninterrupted. When all feels like it is spinning out of control, take heart. Simply pause and be still. *He* is not absent from this moment. *His* eyes are constantly watching, while *His* ears are forever listening. *He* is present in this situation. When panic creeps-in and fear walks-out, don't let that pave an avenue to your soul. When desperation overwhelms and despair tries to take ahold, don't stand in the shadows, grasping at control. Step into *The Light*! Know that *God* foresaw this coming long ago. *He* is not lost in any chaos, nor is *He* incapable of helping us. Through all storms *He* is prevailing. *His* mission is one of eternal restoring and saving. Oh, do not fear little flock, for *God* has overcome this world!

Yes, there is uncertainty, and yes there is confusion – these things are to be expected. Questions will linger without answers and circumstance can lack your understanding, but do not let this be a reason to doubt. *He* is *The King of all Creation*! *His* wisdom far surpasses any comprehension. *He* knows exactly what is happening and exactly where things are going. *His* hands have not been idle; *His* will is not hollow. *He* is always building. Remember who *He Is*! *He* is *The God of the Imaginable – The Lord of Highest Glory – The Host of Heaven's Armies*. Oh, do not fear little flock, for *God* has overcome this world!

Days can blur and unease does not rest. But you should. Concerns will mount and leaders will stumble. But you should remain calm. Anxieties will erupt and knees will tremble. But you should not worry because *He* is still true – true to *His* word and true to *His* nature. This world will wait, afraid to be vulnerable, but you are protected because you are *His* loving adoration. *His* courage *He* gives us; *His* hope defends us. Our *Savior* washes our feet with *His* own hands, and so too will our worries be washed away by those same hands. Oh, do not fear little flock, for *God* has overcome this world!

Run! Run like the child within. Run like the wind that surrounds him. Throw your hands in the air. Run without any care. Joyfully chase your brothers and gleefully race your sisters. Allow your mind to again wonder! Allow your hearts to again pursue the love of others! Live free – play, sing! Stand fast in this moment, firmly embracing this minute. Let your lives work as if they knew no regret. Let your eyes see the beauty of living for today. Release the inner child you've been shielding; release the inner one you've been hiding. You are *His* calling. You are *His* treasure. *He* died for you to have freedom, here now and forever. Oh, do not fear little flock, for *God* has overcome this world.

Let the mighty raise their fist to shout, where the humble have lowered their heads to bow. Let the bold tell you "watch out!" But let the meek proclaim, "*You* are what this is all about!" This is not an end, but a beginning – a transition with which *He* can be trusted. Cast your fears to the side. Sweep them away with careless pride. Bring your hopes upon *His* Son, for *He* has paid your ransom – each and everyone. Life is more then what you know; life is more than what you think. *Heaven* is over the horizon and *He* is there patiently watching and waiting. You are *His* chosen; hand-picked before you were born. You are *His* children; nothing can prevent *His* love from overflowing. Oh, do not fear little flock, for *God* has overcome this world!

HOPELESS

*L*ord, without *You* I am hopeless. Without *You* I am helpless too. My significance is only in *You*, not in me. My time on earth is brief and my ability to get-by depends on navigating the unseen. I stumble from moment to moment. I manage minute by minute. There are no guarantees. This world is not my home, it is simply where I was born.

But *God, You* are my maker. *You* are my creator too. I am just an empty vessel. My life on its own is helpless, my soul hopeless. My body is frail – even at its strongest, it is only temporary. My time and my strength will indeed run out. I cannot endure forever. Even still, *You* provide the way. *You* provide the substance too. Each day is a gift. Each hour is a blessing. Each minute is an honor. Each second should be counted.

Lord, I rest in *You*. I cannot help it. I am overwhelmed by the truth and I am helpless against it too. But for it I am hopeless. The truth is, I am no match for this world. I am not wanted anymore then the next – any less than the last. I am just existing, walking in a circle until my circle is drawn to a close. To the next person, I am just an obstacle. To the last person, I am just a passerby. When measured by others, this life does not measure-up.

But *God, You Yourself* are the promise. And I cling to that promise too. *You* give hope and I am encouraged. *You* give help and I am thankful. To *You* I have purpose. My plans are in *Your* capable hands. *You* know that I am weak – *You* know that I am broken. *You* love me anyways. *You* call me *Your* child. *You* love me fully. *You* don't need me, but *You* want me. I am grateful for *Your* generosity. *You* are good too. There is no other. *You* are *The King*!

Lord, every breath is a new awakening. Every heartbeat is a steady reminder too. Life is only in *You – Your hands – Your feet – Your side*. *You* wore a crown of thorns so I could wear one of gold. *You* walked a road of dirt so I could walk one richly paved. *You* bore sin so I would not bear shame. From eternity past *You* choose me. I didn't choose *You*. *You* are *The Savior* who is, who was, and who will be forever! Oh, without *You* I am hopeless; without *You* I am helpless too!

But *God, You* are my rescue. *You* are my redeemer too. I will trust *You* in the dead of night. I will trust *You* when I've lost my sight. *You*, who forgives my sin. *You* who has shown mercy so that I may live. Not one hour or one breath goes unnoticed by *You*. Not one step or one stumble too. *You* guard me through and through. *You* are *My Helper – My Hope – My Light*. *Your* hands are mighty, and *Your* arms do keep. Not a single circumstance is outside *Your* control or beyond *Your* reach. So, this day I surrender. This day and forever. Help me to be a man after *Your Heart* – nothing more, nothing less, nothing else that would lead us apart.

4

TRUST AND FAITH

*T*rust and Faith is specific to highlighting the weakness within the mind and strengthening it through reinforcing examples of *God's* friendship and companionship. At one time or another, everybody needs to be reminded that *God* is in control. These writings dedicate their message to this central truth.

The Steps of a Man
The Big Picture
If I Knock
Faithful
The Road Worn Before
As a Father
The Heart of Me
Contentment

THE STEPS OF A MAN

*T*he steps of a man are his alone to take; they were not meant for another. They tell the tale of his life lived, and the distinct journey through it. Every footprint made is a deliberate marker in time, although many were left by accident with the temporary only in mind. Some will be regretted. Still others celebrated. Truly the steps of a man cannot be replicated.

The steps of a man travel far and stretch him wide; he does not tread them lightly. Over mountaintops they climb and through valleys crawl. They are refining by their nature. Some reach high with victory, while others fall low in defeat. This is to be expected. For each forms a pillar of deeper understanding – setting the foundation upon which his life has been building. Certainly, the steps of a man are measured. They can be counted, but they are far too heavy to be weighed!

The steps of a man can become confusing; frustrating when he lets them. Because inevitably they will stumble over obstacles he never foresaw coming. In these moments his answers will be few, with the questions mounting. His heart will ache, feeling abandoned by its purpose. And as he collects his scattered thoughts from among the broken pieces of his logic. He'll fail to make sense of it all, causing his confidence to waver. Yes, the steps of a man can leave him lost, hopeless if he allows it.

The steps of a man were known long before he was born; they are not accidental. Their placement in this world is precise, planted perfectly between the thorns and the rose petals. There he is free to bloom outright and unobstructed. Learning to walk by trust, even when he knows not where he's going. In this garden, he is nourished from the rains of *Heaven's* own fountain. Where in its mist he beholds *God's* plan, holy and eternal. Out of such beauty and pain, surrender reveals itself as to why he was created. Surely the steps of a man are directed, guiding him exactly where he was intended.

The steps of a man are not all perfect, but all are forgiven. For there is nothing he can do that is ever beyond the love of his *Father*. His trespasses and his transgressions, each are erased completely. From the record they will fade – no longer to be remembered. His stains and his mistakes, neither is condemning. Since it's only in our failings that *God's* grace is demonstrated unending – and in *His* mercy, compassion delivered undeservedly. Thankfully, all the steps of a man are redeemed, victorious through his *Savior*!

THE BIG PICTURE

"To see the big picture," you have to look beyond the focal point, even beyond the frame. You have to be willing to step back, and gaze from a distance at something in the distance. Your perspective must be broad. To limit your attention to the confined, coarse collection of colors constrained on the canvas, only allows the mind to constrict upon that which is clear and apparent at the time, foregoing the splendor of the experience and rendering the big picture to the lost recesses of wonder. Actually, the artwork is not the astonishment. Instead, the amazement is something bigger – grander. To truly see the big picture, you must "un-see" the obvious, and look to the obscured.

For a lifetime, a man will attempt to gather understanding and solace by looking directly into the depiction, seeing each dab of color and each boldly raised line. He will examine in awe its precision, believing the dimensions are calculated and measured. But in truth, as he peers, he merely only hopes it to be so deliberate. And, although as beautiful and exquisite as each construct can be, it is interwoven intimately between the surrounding hues, intricately dependent on the existing illumination in order to achieve the individual purpose – presenting a realistic representation. Ironically, despite the conclusions of many, the beauty does not stand alone. It is contingent upon something more.

When viewing a masterpiece, one must in fact not simply evaluate the art and its image, but include the artist and his intent. The biggest misconception in "seeing the big picture" is to believe the painting alone encompasses completion. It doesn't. The observer stares intently at the display, awaiting the moment of profound awakening; expecting to behold a prophetic understanding that will ease the plight of life. But rather, he is left abandoned by inspiration's elusiveness, failing to feel "fulfilled" and all too aware of his frailty. He desperately wants to find meaning and direction, and so turns desperate when he does not. He neglects to realize it is *The Creator* who provides context and clarity to the collaboration. Only by looking upon *Him* will "the big picture" become fully evident. Only by surrendering his dependence of personal reasoning, will his mind unbind and his eyes un-blind – allowing the scales of ambiguity to fall.

"Seeing the big picture" rests upon relying on *The Designer*, who crafted the creation, to designate its significance in conjunction with *His* own. *He* alone bestows magnificence. The picture in itself cannot provide the understanding necessary to negate life's difficulties and navigate its currents. But, by believing in *His* ability, knowing *His* goodness, and trusting in *His* promises, will the shackles that restrain mankind to worrying in the unseen, be released – no longer able to hold captive the concerned. A resounding faith in *His* hands to be true, *His* pallet to be pure, and *His* intentions to be noble, soothes the eager onlooker's searching soul and ultimately makes perceiving the big picture possible. The big picture can indeed be mysterious, but thanks to the benevolent nature of *The Painter*, it can be accessible, discernible and observable. *His* glorious presence settled beside the portrait and *His* eternal fingerprint embedded within the print, is what we can depend on for guidance and peace for an eternity and a day.

Stated plainly, "To see the big picture" is impossible without seeing the one who holds the brush!

"To those who are desperate; to those who are ready to surrender. Hang on, hope is on the horizon. Look past the present. His skills are overwhelming, running deep, and His plan is to forever provide. Take comfort, the picture is still being painted – it is not yet finished. But when it is, it will make perfect sense and a lifelong pursuit by a God who loves you will be imprinted upon your heart and within the landscape of your life."

IF I KNOCK...

If I knock, will you answer? Won't you stop to look around? For I bring you good news! There is an awakening. From death, life has found the humble and the proud.

If I declare, will you listen? Do you know of what glorious splendor awaits? Truly I offer you a Heavenly home filled with marvel and majesty, accompanied by a life-long relationship not forsaking mercy, availability, or grace!

If I knock, will you answer? Do you know who I am? My name is Yahweh, The Lord God Almighty, who runs to rescue the decent alongside the damned!

If I declare, will you listen? Rejoice, I have come to set all captives free! And my blood does not discriminate, but instead washes away the stain of every prisoner's conviction — releasing each from regret to soar high on eagles' wings!

If I knock, will you answer? Did you know this is not the place where our journey starts? But rather, I have been watching you, providing for you, loving you since before you were born. My child, you hold a very special place in my heart!

If I declare, will you listen? Make no mistake you are my

chosen creation of love. Cast in my image and forged through my pain, nothing is more exquisite on earth, below, or above!

If I knock, will you answer? Oh, your face is that treasure which I long to see! Shining, radiating, glowing, smiling in Heaven for nothing short of an eternity!

If I declare, will you listen? Do not be confused, this world is not your home. It only cherishes hollowness – the idols of man's invention – placing them on a shallow, superficial, underserving throne.

If I knock, will you answer? To what will be your reply? Life guarantees just a series of fleeting moments and if you wait too long, this holy gift will have patiently, yet predictably passed you by.

If I declare, will you listen? I beg you, do not respond in delay! Faithfully, my plan has been in motion since the beginning of time, and these precious minutes today, are slowly, quietly, quickly, forever ticking away.

If I...

'KNOCK'... 'KNOCK'... 'KNOCK'...

FAITHFUL

*W*hat does it mean to be faithful, and how will I know when I am? This question constantly drifts through my mind, just as a branch floats along the stream's glossy surface, carried by the current's call to the sea. Am I everything *You* want me to be? Am I living a life that pleases *You*? The questions mount. My mind is scared but my spirit bold, so why is my faith not always strong, though I wish it to be? I wonder. I yearn to trust unquestionably. Will that day ever come? Will I always have doubts, or one day, will my doubts disappear?

What does it mean to be faithful, and how hard will this life be? If I am faithful, will my trying times evaporate into the unknown – will my life's plan unfold clearly, marking exactly which turns to make and which directions to take? How long will I wander, searching for understanding? Can a faithful man question the reasons behind the troubling season? Am I fair in asking for an end to my fight, or do I say nothing and calmly await the day of reconcile? Where can I find help; where can I find hope? My questions now multiplying, all I need is an answer. Will *You* please reveal just a little so I can know a lot?

Quietly I wait for a reply, and quietly I do hear one...

Faithful is walking blindly but seeing who leads. Like the blinded beggar who could "see" the truth but not the way, and the followers who could "see" the way but had a blinded heart to the truth.

Faithful is surrendering when you cannot stand and surrendering when you can — trusting that the purpose of living is to purposely allow You control of my life.

Faithful is forging ahead through foreign terrain, not knowing where the path leads but knowing the path has been charted since before time.

Faithful is losing your way, only to find you were on the right path from the very beginning.

Faithful is releasing grip of your dreams and ambitions to pursue the goals of a God you have never seen or spoken to face-to-face.

Faithful is using your God given talents for God's own glory, purpose, and service with no regret.

Faithful is letting go of control, only to realize you never were in control in the first place.

Faithful means trusting the God who controls the universe to manage the simple affairs of a single man's life.

Faithful is not knowing the answers, but still posing the questions and trusting God to point the way.

I am not a preacher or pastor, saint or soldier. I am just an ordinary man who is living from day to day. Like many others, I am trying to just make it moment-by-moment, trying to figure out how and if I will be able to make it through this day. My interests are simple, coming from a sincere heart. The world watches and waits for me to fall, and inevitably I will fall. But being faithful means trusting I will get up and return stronger than before. I will keep praying because there is a *God* who is in control. In the midst of brokenness and chaos, I will fall on bended knees and believe everything is going according to *His* plan. So, although I am not always sure, I will continue to battle and begin to trust.

Faith is about trust. I will trust *You* to deliver me through my stormy trial. I will trust *You* to lead me along the narrow path. I will trust that *You* know what *You* are doing. And I will trust that *You* have not forgotten me. Trust is the key that unlocks the chest of peace; and trust is the key I will carry in my heart until it is my time to open *Heaven's* glorious gate. Trust is the key *You* have given to me. Trust is the key that will set me free. Even if no reprieve is granted me, I trust *You* will use my distress for *Your* holiness.

What started out as a single question, erupted into a battery of tormenting inquiries. Questions are the inner drive of mankind. Questions force men into the unknown, and for me, questions have inevitably brought me home. Questions are a natural response of humanity and questions have led to my redeeming peace – peace that now surrounds me.

I came to *You* with a query, and I leave with a resolution. Where fear had held me captive, faith has released my chains and rendered me hopeful. During this time of exploring and soul searching, many questions have been unearthed. Thankfully, though, I believe I have uncovered my remedy. I don't know exactly what faithful is supposed to look like, nor do I know what it should sound like, but I do believe, in the stillness of this moment, I have uncovered truth and trust, thus finding my faithfulness.

THE ROAD WORN BEFORE

*T*he road worn before echoes voices that are no more. The sounds of the lost; the sounds of the scared. Each surface loudly, still no one is there. He who came has went, and he who comes is yet to be sent. But for now, it is my turn to see what life has in store, lying down the road worn before.

I begin the walk by stepping onto the path. The first choice of many in which I will be asked. The challenges rising with each new stride – never ceasing, just relentless like the ocean's unyielding tide. The uncertainty entangles and the mind it wrangles. Its queries are countless and the unease boundless. This road is not easy, nor is it kind. But it must be traveled, and it is my time.

Fear is quick to come and quick to set, as the Adversary attempts to do his best. Casting a stone into the calm unknown – his tricks are as timeless as they are bold. Exploiting worries that cut more than skin deep. Raising the inquiry, "Can I continue without retreat?" I ponder and wonder am I strong enough to pass the test and move from this life to join the rest. To meet those who wait in glory –

who've treaded that road triumphing before me? Their feet might match the footsteps I now take, but my pathway is different in how it uniquely breaks. What if I fail? What if I faint? Surely this cannot be the plight of the saints?

Although my questions mount, my hope it surmounts, and I am reminded without a shadow of doubt. It is I who is anchored to the *Rock of Truth*. For I abide in *The Vine* who produces good fruit. My confidence is not in me but simply in *He – He* who *Is* and *He* who *Was*. *He* who leads because *He* loves. And despite the foe's devilish intent, he stands no match to *The One* on me who was spent.

Certainly the road will become tiresome, at times look bleak. But all along it is right there, lying beneath my feet. The road can seem unending, and the road can hurt. But it won't last forever, and it won't end on this earth. However twisted, tattered, and torn, this road is no accident – it was casted before I was born. A path the enemy hoped would trip and snag, has been used for a greater purpose, part of a grander plan. All I must do is surrender my pride. Releasing to *Him* all that is inside. For all that's asked is to live faithful and free, foregoing my selfish desires to focus on a glorious eternity.

So just like the others who have gone before me, I too will embrace this life-altering journey. Knowing over time each one left their mark. I too will trust *Him* fully to lead me through the dark. And as I do, my steps become firmer with my sight steadfast. I thank you *God* for I know this road has made me to last. Now with my hopes resurrected, like *The Savior* I adore. I will march bravely and joyfully down the road worn before!

AS A FATHER

*A*s a father guides his child across the street, so too *Lord* are *You* leading me. My hands *You* hold; my steps *You* direct. Although I'm easily distracted by the comings and goings – caught up listening to the breeze while following the bees – *You* are carefully watching. Evaluating my future and my past. Determining which path I should take – which path will last. *Your* wisdom is what I need. *Your* understanding is essential to the things I cannot see. Each are critical for my walk. Each are necessary in order for me to cross. As a father guides his child across the street, *Lord* it is *You* who I need.

This world is unforgiving, and its pains are unrelenting, but *You* partner with us. *You* walk alongside, reassuring that we're not alone. This is the truth I cling to. This is the reality I turn to. *You* catch my tears and chase away my fears. *You* are *The King* who rescues from the flame and restores in our moments of shame. When weakness prevails, let *Your* strong arms unveil – hold me near. When temptations surround, let *Your* unbending *Will* abound – lead me away. As a father guides his child across the street, please walk beside me.

Often, I am unsure how to proceed. I cannot foresee what is to come, and I cannot predict how I will respond. But *You* can be counted upon. *You* are good! *Your* ways are true because they come from a heart that is true – true love. I know that *You* care, and I believe that *You* are always there. All I need to do is follow and *You* will show me the way. As a father guides his child across the street, *You* keep me safe.

From one day to the next, I will learn to trust. I will not always succeed, but I will keep trying and seeking. I will face those obstacles that I didn't anticipate, and I will surely encounter those I brought upon myself. Neither can be avoided, and neither should be. They are important in my growth – not just here on earth but as I step into forever. Certainly, my time on earth will pass and my days in this life will become complete. Inevitably I will step into eternity, and thankfully *You* will be there waiting. Just as a father guides *His* child across the street!

THE HEART OF ME

*T*he heart of me has a disease. It is plagued. Within it, forgetfulness runs rampant. I feel helpless to it and, because of it, I am walking in circles. My soul feels under siege. When new challenges surface, all I can think of is the impending doom. I have a lifetime of answered prayers, but strangely they all seem lost in my absent-mindedness. Inside the heart of me the sickness continues to spread as my painful recollections become more ancient and benign.

Truly I say the heart of me has amnesia. The times *You* have been there for me; the things *You* have done. Sadly, I fail to recall. How *You* have redeemed me – when *You* reached down and saved me. I simply overlook. Where mercy had restored, my mind has wondered away. The revelation revealed in the agony has been trampled by the ticking of time. And now, when trials emerge all I can hear is the panicked beat of my own chest. Instead of feeling anchored, I find myself feeling adrift.

The heart of me has memories, but they are quickly fleeting, and their wounds have scarred over. Subsequently, without the pain, I forget the hurt. Without the hurt, I forget the fear and quickly run recklessly into the wonderment of life, where I again find myself facing the fire – reaching to touch the flame. A once refreshing perspective is now over-shadowed by a staleness of peace, and my heart loses the razor's edge of divine awareness that it once held.

Why? Is it a condition of my humanity, or a self-centered reaction to my simple-minded conclusions?

The truth is it probably is a combination of both: an infection of the mind, fed by imperfection, pride and arro-gance combining with an overwhelming influence of worldly stimulus, which drowns the archives of my memory banks with each new daily encounter. Add to this my ever-thirsting search for knowledge, which is easily deceived by the *Great Deceiver*, who implants independence with illogic, masked behind my human desire to freely live as one oblig-ated to nothing or no one. (Consequently, this is the same mindset which led to his fall to begin with.) Together these conditions create obstacles in which my spirit sees despair rather than opportunity for accomplishment.

Clearly my heart stands no chance against its natural gravitation toward deterioration and the supernatural colli-sion of deception and deviation.

Worry not though! In *Your* heart is where healing and hope from my ailment hinge – not mine! *Your* heart is what rescues. *Your* heart is what repairs. *You* transcend *Heaven*, Hell, and ALL in between. For *You*, this world and its enemy are no match and time offers no test.

These poignant truths are what I must emphatically cling to in order to re-capture the chronicles of my past life and produce a future of lasting encouragement. I must purposely ponder on the many times of *Your* provision to allow the heart of me to become emboldened and unafraid.

Only by a concentrated effort to focus on *The One* who knows my plight and still says, *"Come with me, my burden is light,"* will I be able to justly march into life's new ordeals.

Thus, I will resolve to reflect on *You*, inscribing each of *Your* victories on the walls of my heart. In so doing, I am pledging to never forget, but more importantly, by engraving *Your* name on my heart's lining, it ensures the heart of me will forever remember *You*.

CONTENTMENT

The mind will not find peace on its own; it will not find contentment alone. It will roam if you let it. Stray if you allow it. Wander until its wonderment is no more. But still, it will lack satisfaction. Those who have tried, know this. Those who have not, will find this so.

Life casts its lure towards the unknown, causing humanity to search for desires untold. We run towards the rainbow but are never able to catch it or its elusive pot of gold. The days evaporate and slowly we discover we are no closer to our hopes than when we first began our pursuit.

The plague of serenity is that it is never where you think it should be found. There is a struggle within the mind – a yearning for that which it does not possess and growing disenchantment for that which it does. The spirit is capable of contentment, just not content with it. What we have will sustain, but sadly it will not fulfill.

Contentment, however, begs us to wrestle with the present. Identifying what we have as the treasure to behold. Sometimes it doesn't sparkle from every ray of light, but its brilliance lies in seeing its natural worth. The gift of today is it is the only thing we are guaranteed to have. We waste the fleeting moments searching for hidden beauties, rather than partaking in our obtained favors. The truth is binding, whether we recognize it or not.

The beauty of living is appreciating the mission of being alive and accepting our circumstances – looking around, breathing in the peace and tranquility of *God's* creation and *God's* provision. Our moments are given hour by hour – breath by breath. Accept the uniqueness of you and your circumstances. They shaped your sense of self. *God* is a master designer. *He* does not make mistakes. Trust *His* divineness and strength. *He* loves unmeasurably and *His* might is incomprehensible. *He* does not fail! The reality is this is the only life we have. We can't wish it away and shouldn't waste it away either. It's only when we look to *The Source,* can we find true peace and everlasting fulfillment. I have all I need because I have *Who* I need! Accept the Surrender!

5

DIRECTION AND SURRENDER

irection and Surrender engages a man's will versus his understanding. All too often, humans are questioning which direction to go and who should be leading. The world claims a man's destiny is determined by him alone, but *God's Truth* makes another declaration. It calls men to yield to their *Creator*, and these writings help the reader to see the divine compass points on the "Map of Life."

The Captain of His Destiny
Light Overtakes the Darkness
Deeply
The Direction
The Uncertainty of Going
Surrender
The Journey
What's a Man to Do?
My Commitment to Surrender

THE CAPTAIN OF HIS DESTINY

The waters were calm when first I did set out. My vision was clear – there was not one single cloud. My cares were few with my worries to match. Nothing could stop me; nothing would hold me back. For I was The Captain, and this life was mine to own! The world had no bars, I would claim that which I was owed. With pride as my companion and confidence our guide, victory was certain. There was only treasure to find. Yes, good fortune awaited, in this I truly believed. I was bound and determined, destined to be!

Oh, how the ocean was inviting the farther along I went. My ambitions became intoxicating, a thirst that wouldn't let me relent. I sailed onward without hesitation, "Tell me why would I not?" "Nothing will rob me of this destiny," I assuredly thought. For I am The Captain, and this ship is under my command! This journey is about fate; besides, things are going just as I planned.

But the winds they shifted. Subtly they did change. No longer were they welcoming – the air became cold, bitter, and strange. And a new sound arose, coming from across the great unknown. It was hollow and ancient, beckoning me with its desperate moan. Whoa, for the first time I felt scared. For the first time I felt weak. For the first time I felt helpless, as I watched my confidence abandon when panic did inward creep. Yes, I was afraid, of this I could be sure. Because vulnerability was a feeling I'd not felt before. Still my ego was stubborn – it wouldn't let me slow. In defiance it shouted boldly, "You are The Captain! Never let the doubt within you show!"

Yet the waves they pounded, unrelenting with their attack. Crashing they battered, until my pride stumbled, and I began to crack. Into pieces I was broken; just a man left scattered amongst his wreck. Under the weight of humility I was drowning, submerged by life's painful regret. Into icy waters I was tossed, like a lure I was cast. Powerless I couldn't stop the momentum; against its wake I didn't stand a chance. Where once I proclaimed to be The Captain, and so proud to boast of this! Really, I was just a passenger, holding his ticket to life's inevitable abyss.

Down I went without stopping, my desires all but a stolen memory. The future I had so desperately longed for, would now damn me straight into eternity. Those treasures of life I hunted; the ones to which I did hungrily cling. To my grave they will forever imprison – like shackles, they are bound to never let me leave. Arrogance it became my anchor and pride was to my shame. The gates of Hell the only thing for me waiting! "Oh Captain," they devilishly taunted, "for your destiny you have only yourself to blame!"

And while I was still sinking, alone to face the end. A hand reached into the darkness and began pulling, fighting to free me from the grave reeling me in. I felt *Him* grasp me firmly, and I saw the scars upon *His* wrists. Battle marks that foretold a ransom – purchasing salvation – my life in exchange for *His*. Against certain death *He* wrestled, and against my own life's waywardness *He* did not condemn. When justice demanded my guilty verdict, *He* simply said, "Child, I forgive." Yes, *He* rescued me from the deep of deep, and how deeply grateful was I! My life was returned from damnation. My destiny undisputed, I was alive! So now whenever I think about my journey and recall all the places I'd been. It's clear each time that I thought I was The Captain I was wrong. It was always and only *Him*!

LIGHT OVERTAKES THE DARKNESS

*T*he sun slips into the sky, past the on-looking horizon exposing the terrain. The landscape stretched before me is bold and distinct, yet my walk is clearly undefined. Every turn I consider charters a different course. With each new decision mounting, I know repercussions are patiently waiting. I close my eyes slowly and open them suddenly. I am blinded. The light overtakes the darkness.

I move about my day and the shadows sway, conforming and disguising themselves amidst the changing hours. Challenges emerge and uncertainty is ever certain. Some choices are clear, while others were clearly wrong. Which will have a lasting effect, and which will be laughed aside? I stumble from moment to mishap, momentum to misstep – rising and falling with each stride. I wonder. I can't help but wonder. Will the light overtake the darkness?

Distrust and worry settle deep. My spirit is restless. The fear of insecurity incased in ambiguity, accompanied by deception, scatters my strength. How can I be expected to discern what's undiscovered? I am merely a man trying to sift through this vast obscurity and forge ahead towards *destiny*. Much is at stake, unfairly placed on an unqualified soul. Strangely, I sense twilight encroaching in midday. A breaking point is reached, when from above, in the form of love, relief rains down gently. And with it, the light again overtakes the darkness.

"Never once did I leave you on your own. Never once did you ever walk alone," echoes from across the cosmos and into my conscious thought. These softly spoken words sing loudly, seizing my attention, grabbing ahold of my frailty – transforming my faith. *"Is your unmarked path still not a path deliberately made?"* This question from *On-High* resounds to me below, and I recognize although my future thus far is unseen, it is not unwritten. Just as every work of art begins as a simple depiction, the coveted masterpiece only awaits new strokes of color to illuminate previously unrevealed patterns of brilliance. *The Creator* has confirmed in *His* creation. Shadows cannot hide on a canvas fully exposed. The light always overtakes the darkness.

I rest. I am relieved. What began without direction, I now realize never actually went without guidance. In time what was unknown became known; what was untold is now told. Despite The Deceiver's attempts to discourage and devoid the world of sight, truth forever radiates brightly from *The Son – The Promised One –* who conquered death and dismay. In *Him*, hope is restored. In *Him*, pleas are not ignored. In *Him*, the lost are found. And, in *Him*, evil shall not abound! Halleluiah, *The Light of the World* has overtaken the darkness!

I wake-up to a new day and a new dawn. Where to go? What to do? The options are endless! This journey is once more underway as I step from the four walls where I slept. I look to the east – awestruck I watch! I cannot help but watch, as the light overtakes the darkness!

DEEPLY

*L*ord allow me to know *You* deeply – unconditionally, with genuine, whole-hearted feeling. Help me to obey *Your* commands freely and listen to *Your* voice completely. *You* alone are *The God of the Universe*, who reaches down daily to touch us. *You* travel beside and within; upholding, never failing to offer riches of abundance. Although this world *You've* designed declares its own significance, *You* have solemnly promised an everlasting friendship. *You* offer a relationship personal in its conception – fully satisfied within *Your* planned purpose. For this reason, I desire a closer connection. I wish to be surrendered in total commitment. Please grant me a willing mind and an understanding spirit, reinforced with a courageous heart and an outreaching hand of service. Let my worldly affirmation to others bestow, "The deeper *You* ask me to follow, the more deeply I shall seek to go!"

Lord I recognize I do not always know *Your* will, but confidently I say I do know *Your* ways. History has recorded *Your* deeds throughout time and its days. Past moments of mercy display timeless lessons of grace. And individual encounters of revelation reveal we were never abandoned in an undetermined chase. *Your Word* teaches *You* never forget or forsake those who depend on *You* with undying love. In fact, *You* uphold them from *Your* mighty kingdom – high, high above. As *You* sit enthroned, forever reigning. They are the branches *You* nourish with a sweet, *He*avenly downpouring. Why I ask, do *You* show us such glorious favor? The answer is simple – *Your* agenda has always been a vision of grandness and splendor! A timeless message the prophets of past each foretold, "The deeper I shall seek to go, the more deeply *You* connect me to *Your* soul!"

Lord inspired I am now ready to shadow *Your* lead – to become that person *You've* created me to be. All I request is that along the way *You* remain as my life's centerpiece. Resounding from my every footstep, like a marching parade's guiding drumbeat. Make love the single intention of my every action. Forging within me a drive to reach far into eternity – grasping. Holding *Your* words firm – tightly with conviction. And living-out-loud in boldness, comprehension, and compassion. Oh, to the *God* whose affection is unsurpassed, I owe *You* all I have, all I had, and all I ever will clasp. Sow in me today what only tomorrow *You* can reap. Harvest fruit of the spirit, heart, mind, and strength – my everything. For I rest assured, "The deeper *You* connect me to *Your* soul, the more deeply I will love *You* and wholeheartedly follow!"

THE DIRECTION

*W*hich direction do I go? I often ask. Am I on the right path? I wonder at that. Is there a map to life, marking where to turn? Or perhaps a sign in a language I haven't yet learned. How do I know when I have arrived? Who will tell me? What will I find? Am I standing in line, like those awaiting an amusement park ride? Or should I grab the wheel, and be my own guide? This earthly journey is complicated, and its street not paved. So what bumps in the road can I expect along my way?

As I look all around, many choices I see. Each pulling and tugging – beckoning me. Too many decisions; too little time. If I answer incorrectly will I move backwards in stride? Miles behind where I youthfully began. Still no closer to a successful and pleasant storybook end. Perhaps, forever altering what happiness had in store, or will joy hang-on, and wait patiently as it had before?

With so many questions, it's as clear as can be. The answers aren't simple, and they definitely aren't easy. I once thought it wise to ask a close friend. But now I'm not certain. For what do they know – where have they been? Companions are good but they too have their doubts. Wondering what this world is really all about. Despite their best intentions, the solutions they offer are only temporary fixes. Not something I can depend upon permanently for my detailed predicaments.

However, just when I think I'm entangled within my own thoughts. Strangely enough a glimpse of awareness dawns in the surfaces of the rough. In spite of all the ambiguity, some insights emerge strikingly clear. In fact, they are not so distant, but rather very, very near. These certainties ring as loudly and boldly as ever, and they are the facts we must cling to, securing as our treasures...

The trees will grow, and the birds will nest. The sun will rise, and the sun will set.

No matter how large a cloud in the sky appears, the blue can always be seen by at least someone, sometime, somewhere.

Seasons will come and seasons will go, as time continues its march to and fro.

Spring brings green and autumn yields brown. But people sadly race through their days, missing all the beauty by rarely looking around.

The mountains are tall. The ocean is vast. And pain is temporary, it will not last.

Love will conquer hate, and evil will not win. Because God is reigning in Heaven – the same place He has always been.

Life is unique and its stories demonstrate the same. Each of us has a purpose and an eternal flame. But we all fall victim to the devilish scheme – worrying about tomorrow, instead of enjoying this day's scene. How much do we miss by looking past today? Questioning and hoping to control what is not a given anyway. We spend our moments plotting and charting a course, that can all be taken away abruptly by just a single source. A poor decision here, or a collective one there; or even an act of nature, none of which will care. Yes, our worrying is wasted on the things unknown, instead of a focused peace spent growing faithful and gracefully growing old.

The truth is "the secret to life" is not a secret at all. It's not a shadow hiding on the wall. It's not a reflection that quietly disappears. But strangely a splendor of wonder, more defined by its years. It is spelled out eloquently for all to see. It is available to you who look – and also to me. Abundant living is not about avoiding your plight, but reaching out your wings, preparing to take flight. Contrary to what many think death is not what we should fear, rather it is living a life empty and void of the *Loving Savior*.

So, when you find yourself facing a fork where the road once ran straight. Or perhaps you're now at a standstill, staring at an insurmountable gate. In these moments I tell you, cling to what you know. The reality that has been revealed deep within your soul. Although uncertainty may leave you feeling betrayed and on your own. You have not been abandoned, nor will you go it alone. Life is a building block, each day upon another – culminating in a deeper recognition that produces a rewarding life-long endeavor. Just remember *time* provides the context for the voyage to define. Thus, when despair sets in and challenges arise, look *Up* not forward, sideways, or behind.

THE UNCERTAINTY OF GOING

*D*o you have to know where or when, or can you just go? Should you feel compelled to move, or do you just walk through any open door? What about what was? Is it to be overshadowed by what will be? Must I know why I'm leaving, or can I leave that to the uncertainty of going?

Do you have to see who is leading or can you trust in the unseen? Do you have to hear a calling or is the silence beckoning? Do you have to be invited by name or are all included? If you were content in your ways, should you venture into the vast unknown? Were you meant to leave, or can you leave that to the uncertainty of going?

Do you need to start where the path begins, or can you step in line anywhere along the way? Must you march at the front, or can your journey come from behind? When the track becomes twisted, should you continue-on in spite? Or is this an indication of an apparent and absolute end? When the trail is at a crossroad, should you blindly pick a path? Or simply stand-fast, waiting for an undeniable determination? When the road becomes darkened, should you wait for a light, or instead muddle your way through the shadows? Do you have to know where you are going, or can you leave that to the uncertainty of going?

If you've asked for guidance, can you rest assuredly there will be a guide? Should you stay where you have always known, or should you step into the strange? Will you become lost or is lost the direction you were supposed to be going all along? Must you know who is leading, or can you leave that to uncertainty of going?

What is the harm in trying? What is the harm in failing? What is the pain in falling? What is the pain in recreating? What is the error in asking? What is the error in assuming? Which is correct; which is incorrect? When you have more questions than answers can you afford to risk leaving, or can you leave that to the uncertainty of going?

The truth is the uncertainty of going is really the uncertainty of "not knowing." Not knowing is the hurdle that must be overcome – the obstacle that must be mastered. Not knowing causes anxiety and not knowing moves feelings of fear. Not knowing is paralyzing and not knowing is penetrating. Not knowing causes us to focus on the temporary. And not knowing causes us to ignore the truths on which we can depend.

Ironically though, uncertainty is the signal of saving grace. Because of it, we are moved to surrender and then to dependence upon a guiding hand as timeless as the ages – as faithful as the seasons – as dependable as the tide. This palm holds us and this name, in-turn we have engraved on our hearts. The uncertainty of going can be concerning, but it is truly the only certain way to seek the *"Author and Director of Going."*

We need to be able to rest in the midst of uncertainty because that is where *God* reveals *His* intentionality. Our faith is an expression of our trust, and our trust is tested in the moments of uncertainty. We all too often look at the waves. But *God* helps us to walk upon the waves and prompts us to live without wondering. Uncertainty will ultimately become a way of life because it will develop a comfort that *He* certainly is in control.

In spite of the complex questions, a simple one surfaces, *"Where have you sought – to whom do you ask?" He* is *The One* who guides and directs the steps of those who whole-heartedly seek *Him. He* will not let them fall. *He* holds them by the hand. If you have pursued *Him*, then step boldly in any direction, *He* will make your path straight.

> *God*: *"What if I told you I will take care of you,*
> *would you worry?"*
> –Me: "No!"
> *God*: *"Haven't I always taken care of you?"*
> – Me: "Yes, *Lord!"*

SURRENDER?

If *You* ask me to surrender, I will surely say "No,"
If I give it all up, oh what would I have to show?
My hands would become tied
and my feet forced to go,
The road I now walk would quickly grow cold.
For who would remember me
or would even care to know?
I would feel so lost, so alone.
Like on a drifting ship tossed to and fro,
All my worldly possessions
would scatter just as the leaves the wind blows.
My life would seem changed, forever broke,
And that dire fate upon no one
would I wish to bestow.

Why would I choose to surrender?
What good would that do?
Clearly my days of pleasure would be over,
finished, through.
Does anyone know

how an existence like that concludes?
For I say with certainty, I haven't a clue!
I can tell *You* what I do though
– I feel chaos and it looms,
My mind is afraid, my gut dreads doom.
How long would I be gone
and where would I resume?
If I resign power of my being
then I will be controlled by whom?
These are pounding questions
with answers I wish I knew.

Why do *You* ask me to surrender,
what can that mean?
To purposely let it all go
is as terrifying as a frightening dream.
Treading such a course is tiresome
and staying strong is not done with ease,
What's more, I'm scared
– where does it all lead?
Devastation is the only order in store for me,
or so it would seem.
Why does such a request
require such a drastic extreme?
I'm bewildered,
why would *You* even ask such a thing?
You say others have done it
– well that's slightly hard to believe,
How much did they forfeit?
And for me, what is there to possibly achieve?

If I must surrender, why now? Can't it wait?
I'll get to it in due time. I promise, I won' be late.

Besides, my years are already planned
– I've designed my own fate.
What can *You* offer me currently
that I couldn't get at a later date?
You mention a better life
and an inner peace that won't taint,
Why am I so special? What makes me so great?
Aren't there others *You* would rather try to attain?
(Oh, *You* are seeking them too
but at this moment I'm the one on *Your* slate?)
Well, what do *You* require of me then,
and how many of my precious minutes will it take?
(Oh, *You* ask nothing more of me
than to simply not hate,
Love and seek *You,*
and stay rendered to that state.)
That doesn't sound so difficult,
but I can speak confidently
that's not a natural trait.

What if I do surrender,
where can I call my new address?
Will *You* kindly describe
where I'll lay my head to rest?
Your Book boasts of a home marked with indescribable
righteousness,
Streets of Gold and beauty
far too brilliant for anyone to express.
Its landscape is filled with
peace, tranquility, worship, and holiness,
Where I will be surrounded by loved ones
who sing out in uncontrollable joyousness.
To top it all off,

it's offered for an eternity and nothing less,
Please, please, will *You* tell me
if this has been inaccurately assessed?
For I would hate to seek
and find not the pre-described happiness.

(Oh, it is the case and furthermore,
mere words can't bring it full justice.)
Wow, how wonderful and truly marvelous!
I so amazed yet deeply embarrassed,
Because I was convinced my demise
was *Your* only interest.
I doubted *Your sincerity*
– *Your love* –
Your kindness.
For the longest time
I've tried to ignore *Your* single request.
Faithful are *You*
though because *You* are relentless,
You lovingly chased me until I listened,
opening my eyes to witness.
Now I will no longer doubt.
For it's clear, *You* know best.
And when *You* ask me to surrender,
I will surely say "Yes!"

THE JOURNEY

*T*here is one true journey a man will take which will forever shape his life. On this voyage, he will be tested in trials; unearthed by uncertainty; and frozen with fear. His road will become blinding and binding. His eyes burned and blurred – while his steps shaken and strained. He must however endure to the very end in order to reveal his true self. Without the journey, he would go on believing he is who he ought to be. Not until he completes the travel, will he recognize who he was ultimately called to become.

Today is a new day, but for me a new hope quickly fades. The clouds have rolled in. They encircle each other, spawning more and more power and might. They swarm the sun – concealing it – suffocating its glow. Every direction I look reveals darkness and distress. I gaze into the venomous sky, and I realize my journey is now underway.

As I attempt to set out on an uncharted and unknown path, my heart races and my palms sweat. I cannot help but feel frightened and alone. This storm is unlike any other I have witnessed. It reaches far beyond the storm of a decade.

It will most certainly be the storm of a *lifetime*. I ponder what lies at the end of this road, but especially I ponder at what lies alongside it. Regardless of the obstacles, still I know I must go forward. I could choose to stay behind, but I would be held captive – a prisoner to my frustrations – to my faults – and to my failings. There would be no escape. I would remain entrapped within my own body and my own mind; a nomad, unsettled, unfulfilled, and undefined. Left to forever wander and wonder, constantly tormented by my unrelenting desire to become whole but unable to do so. No, I must press on! My very survival depends upon it.

Before I begin though, I must take pause. For I have no idea of which direction to proceed. Each way looks as hopeless as the next, and they all appear to lead to my demise. My strength is quickly fleeting. I feel myself fall to my knees. My heart is begging for help, and so I pray while the words uncontrollably flow from my mouth...

"Oh Lord, I cry out to You in the midst of this terrifying storm, hear me please. This weight is too much to bear. The gale is impossible for me to navigate alone. Please Lord, be my captain – be my guide – be my light. Walk ahead of me and I will follow in Your footsteps; I will step where You step; I will walk where You walk. I do not know which direction to go, but I trust that You do. Please deliver me through the wilderness and through this trying time."

"I am weak, but You are strong and mighty. You give me hope because You are my provider. I take peace in that hope and will one day rest in Your grace. Please be merciful toward me as the clouds enclose around me. Please grant me wisdom as I discern my way through their overwhelming elements. When my footing slips, be

*there to catch me – break my fall. Oh Lord, be The Rock
to which I can cling while the rain and the wind try to
swallow me. Please, do not abandon me. I am a sheep,
lost and desperately seeking a shepherd before the lion
arrives. Hear my voice and be my Savior. Cut through
this darkness and see me to the end."*

*"Everything around me seems to be crumbling. All that I
use to count-on is counted as lost. Victory is fleeing from
my grasp. Help me to understand its true definition, and
the true meaning of living so that I can rise above this
world and not yield to hopelessness. Please give me
endurance to finish the race I have started and finish
it well."*

*"I acknowledge my existence is tenuous – fragile at best.
It is far outside of my control. I further realize much of
my life's consequences are the consequence of my going
alone and not trusting in You. Help me now to surrender
control to the only one who is capable of handling it all –
You! Your hands are proof I can count on You. In your
death, You gave life. You are a true friend and a compas-
sionate Father. My past lack of faith in Your ability to
lead is what has driven me into the heart of this storm.
Now may I trust in You to redeem me and carry me
through it."*

*"Oh Lord, I know You are competent! You are careful to
plot the course of my life to ensure Your name can be
honored. So, I say to You with a sincere heart, use me in
this day for Your glory – whatever that means, wherever
that leads, again and again. Amen."*

At last, I am free to face this epic adventure. I have
sought help, and I can be sure help is on the way! I am confident *You* hear me; confident *You* know my concerns; and

confident *You* will deliver me. I can once again look towards the sky with a rejuvenated spirit. I have an eager anticipation as the clouds continue with their parade. I know some will bring thunder; some will bring rain. But both will bring faith. I will emerge from this journey victorious no matter the outcome. Rest assured, I will have been tried in tribulation, refined by fire, and molded into the man I was destined to be. Finally, I have been born again and branded new.

WHAT'S A MAN TO DO?

*W*hat's a man to do when his life has come to an unexpected standstill? How is he to proceed? His days are not at an end, but his path has indeed run its course. So what is he to think? He can't sit idly by as the world turns and time slips away – can he? Life is too short. Its windows of opportunity are slowly closing, and his youthful ambitions are quickly fading. What is he to do?

What is a man to do when the road he travels is at its end, but his journey is not? What is he to believe? The dreams he chases run wildly from him. They were always just out of reach before – never close enough to be captured – but still close enough to be coveted. Now, they flee into the unknown only to be seen in his dreams. Why are they gone? Where do they hide? It seems that whenever he thinks he is making progress toward his goal, the finish line changes and leaves him in the distance. Will he ever reach his destination?

His thoughts race toward perplexity. Who is he; what is he; and for what in life is he meant? Sadly, there are more questions than answers – more frustrations than findings – more confusion than conclusions.

So, what's a man to do when his life has come to an unexpected standstill?

Strangely, he must stop and stand still, rather than move aimlessly from left to right, shifting like the wind. He needs to pause and wait for a direction to aim – listening – discerning the voice of *God* from the chaos and confusion of his own thoughts. Silence is the sound until a destination is determined. This may take a moment, or it could take many. Fear and failures will attempt to bewilder his mind. But truth and facts must anchor his soul. Emotions cannot overwhelm his heart and suffocate his spirit. A focused perspective will provide peace – a faithful heart will provide relief. And there is only one way to discover these. He must, by being still, rediscover his *Maker*.

Long ago, a pledge was made that a redeemer had promised to provide a pathway; a redeemer had promised to provide peace; and a redeemer had promised simply to provide. Thus, a man must hold tight to this hope of *The Light* and rest through the uncertainty of the night.

To those who might ask, I am he of whom this speaks. My words dawn this page. My distress is inscribed within these lines. I am the man who is lost in the wilderness. I am the one who does not know which way to head. I am the man who worries. And I am the man who wonders, "Why?"

Also, I know I am not alone in my plight. Many share my helplessness. But although, like many I am disorientated, unlike many to which *You* have replied, "Who is this that questions Me?" I say, "I will not be he." For I do know who *You* are. And I do trust that *You* know what *You* are doing. I will hold on until *Your* way is revealed. Although I am weak, in *You* I am strong. Even though I am afraid, in *You* I am calmed.

If you ask the Lord to lead, don't be surprised if you don't know where you are going. His ways are divine – His plan was in-place from before time. Rest assured He knows your needs, but He has a purpose that supersedes our desires. His gracious favor is all we need – it sustains us. We have to surrender whole-heartedly and trust in Him to be God, and for us to be patient.

MY COMMITMENT TO SURRENDER

*M*y commitment to surrender proves daily my toughest commitment to keep. For each day that excellence I strive to achieve, but every night its standard I recognize I've failed to rightly meet. Although my intentions start-off faithful and true, as time elapses my discipline becomes weak and my ambition lacks the necessary follow-through. How does a simple man meet such an esteemed ideal? How does he set aside his selfishness to live for something so surreal? What if he stumbles; what if he fails? Will he forfeit *Your* special favor, or forsake precious *Heavenly* appeal?

My commitment to surrender consistently accounts for my most demanding task. Its obligation to selflessness is tricky to master and my willingness to yield, sadly, it never lasts. Try as I might, my efforts fall short in vain. And when I look around for answers admittedly there's only one – myself – deserving of such blame. Why do I choose this madness? Why do I chase these hollow pursuits? Why do I live a life enslaved in sinful desires – instead of unchained by freedom offered from *The Truth*?

My commitment to surrender is a journey upon which I must not tread lightly. For it is a commission rendered straight from the throne room of *Heaven* to be regarded ever-so highly. It is an undertaking with footsteps carved through painstaking intentionality. And a mission where fingerprints are purposely placed – forever altering. So with that understanding, the course of my life will not again seem inconsequential. As everything I do will have resolve, shining a light upward. I will release control of that which I never did truly hold. To be held by *The One* who promises to never ever let go. I will trust in *His* divine guidance each and every day, ultimately allowing *His Will* to lead my every which way.

My commitment to surrender is a vision I wish to make an actuality. To stand tall in the midst of the crowd of pressing onlookers, boldly and confidently. It's something I want to pursue with renewed determined deliberation, and although I cannot promise perfection, I do promise a heart ripened for fatherly correction. One that accepts *Your* wisdom and reasoning as my mind's sole justification, for whom but *You Oh Lord,* is worthy of such a cherished honor – who but *You Oh Lord,* is so deserving of this objectification with singular reflection? And because *You* did not say "No" to my glaring limitations. I am determined to be reverent of *You* in all things cast my direction. "Thank *You Potter,*" humbly states this clay. "Let my commitment to surrender mean exactly what it says!"

BEFORE YOU GO

*N*ow that you've finished this book, I truly hope your heart has found peace, and your faith is resting in that peace. The purpose of this book was always simply to share *God's* eternal *Truths* of how *He* sees us and to show how much *He* does care. By allowing *His Truth* to resonate into your soul, I'm convinced you will see *The Light* and that light, *Jesus Christ*, will illuminate living in today's world. As light shatters the darkness, so too has *He* overcome the world! This is truth to live by.

When you know *God's Truth*, it provides perspective, which in turn provides peace through every storm. When you know *God's Truth*, you can get up each day refreshed by a new sense of hope and optimism; fully aware of the challenges you will and do face, but equally aware of *The Creator*, who uses those challenges to continually create newly in you. When you know *God's Truth*, fear has no hand to hold and it has no place to hide. Thankfully, *God's Truth* is something that transcends *ALL* – all circumstance, all feelings, all time, all virtual reality – *ALL*! These are *God's Truths* to live by!

The Truth is you are not, and were never meant, to endure life alone. You have not been abandoned! When you discover *God's Truth*, your eyes will be opened, and you will witness life as it was meant to be experienced. *He* is in the boat paddling with you; *He* is standing beside you on the shore; *He* is waiting in the doctor's office next to you; *He* is looking over your finances; and *He* is planning your next meal.

I sincerely thank you for engaging with me in this read! This book comprises *The Cry of My Heart, the Hope of my Faith, and His Response to it All*. I truly appreciate you taking part in this offering. It was an authentic exploration of my heart, mind, soul, and strength bound together upon a page. And as it is with any offering, the intentions behind it are what matter – my intention was always to help. I hope this helped provide perspective and assistance to you in your day-to-day living.

As I close, I would be remiss if I didn't share with you my reluctance to place this "offering" into a public plate – to be passed around for others to view and evaluate. I was nervous about not only my own talent being exposed, but about the act itself. If I am offering *The Lord* my writings, then what right do I have to place that offering anywhere other than in *His* hands? It's a bit philosophical, but it's a genuine reflection of the true dichotomy that I felt. These writings were things *He* helped *me* to compose, and they were moments of quiet time spent between the two of *Us*. They were *His* to use; *His* to share; *His* to do with as *He* pleases – not mine. *He* is the Potter and I am the clay. How could I rightly justify taking such a private moment and turning it into a public display? (Or at least that was what I envisioned I was doing.)

I found myself in an ethical tug-of-war. I had always

believed I was writing to connect with *God*, but also deep-down felt like someone else could benefit from hearing this message. Again, as I described previously in *"Between the Lines,"* these were fictional characters portraying real feelings and learning timeless lessons of *God's Truth*. They taught me, but I also hoped they carried enough weight to reach others. *"Would they lead to any real connection, and was there true depth portrayed upon the pages? What was it that God really wanted me to do with these writings?"*

These were the thoughts that constantly floated through my mind. How could I be an obedient follower if I did not take this dilemma seriously? For years I wrestled with the notion of being true to the act of an offering. Was I being disingenuous by taking what *God* gave me and placing it in the public view? I recalled *Jesus* talking much about similar things. I felt like my reluctance was justified, and these were humble, noble thoughts that I was having – supported biblically.

Yet, in the end, I'm not sure they weren't merely crutches for me to lean upon! If I'm being honest, I think I was really just afraid to bare my soul. (But isn't that the beauty of an offering?) We need to pour out our time, our talent, and our treasure into the offering plate and let *God* multiply, subtract, or merely maintain – to cherish through time as *He* wishes. When you put your offering in the plate its *God's* to use and there's no telling what *He* might do! But unless you put it into the plate you'll never know. It wasn't until a dear friend of mine finally provided me with the necessary perspective I needed that I stepped out in faith with my offering and threw away my crutches.

He and I were having a conversation about this exact topic of publishing this collection of writings into a book. I was explaining to him my reluctance and he casually, but calculatedly stated, "I've never known *God* to ask anyone to keep their lamp hidden under a basket." Wow, in an instant his words penetrated! It dawned on me that this was an example of the exact metaphor *Jesus* was referring to when he talked about letting your light shine; and I was being asked to respond in like manner. Yes, these writings were a personal offering, but they also are an "Act of Worship." And worship, as a public declaration, is powerful!

I don't intend to offend anyone when I say this, but I believe worship has an obvious place in the public square. Worship in its literal form is an expression of a passion, and yes, it certainly does happen in private, but it can, and should, also happen in public too. For in this arena, it has the power to persuade, encouraging others which serves an essential role for fellow believers and the church as whole.

Please, take this testimony and use it to supplement your own. *God* has designed you beautifully and with meaning. Your gifts are an offering to be given to *The One True God*. Maybe you haven't yet discovered your calling, but I urge you, explore! Explore your mind and soul, willing and ready to listen to the *Holy Spirit's* prompting, and then follow *Him* in faith. Jump in with both feet! There's only one way to truly know *God* and that is to make yourself available to *Him* as an offering.

Imagine what this world would be like if we all placed our lamps on a hilltop and waited to see what would happen. My guess is there would be very little darkness! At a time such as this, where disease, devastation, and despair are all around us, the world truly needs your lamp – your community needs your lamp – your workplace needs your lamp – your family needs your lamp! You only have one life and one time to shine, and the truth is, that time in your life is now!

6

ACKNOWLEDGMENTS

*S*pecifically, I want to thank *God* for walking and writing with me these many years. Without *His* help, this book would not have been written and my journey through life would be hopeless, void of direction, peace, and love. *He* is *The Author, The Anchor, The Rock,* and *The Captain* – *My Light* in the Darkness!

Also, I'd like to thank my mom Betty, who has always encouraged me to write. As a child, she said it often, and as an adult she continues to believe in me as a writer. You are a beautiful person whose beauty does not fade. Your words of wisdom and love will impact me forever. Thank you for always listening and supporting me!

To my brothers Justin and Corey, thank you too! Justin you are the one person I trust to understand me completely, and you have counseled me along the way – correcting where necessary and praising accordingly. It has helped greatly! Corey, you have a profound perspective of life that I appreciate more and more each day. I value your input and enjoy your perspective, and I look forward to our future conversations and the enlightenment they will provide!

To Vicky, Crystal and Taylor, each of you has given me help in very unique ways. Vicky your willingness to just "root" for me and support me has been like a harbor in the storm. It is a sanctuary. Thank you! Crystal, your common sense and practical point of view helped me complete this project when I had seemingly reached an impasse. Thank you for your time and willingness to engage, pushing me over the finish line! To Taylor, you were always someone that I wanted to read my writings because I knew if you enjoyed them then they met their intended mark. I always welcome your thoughts and value your time. You provide inspiration and motivation, lifting me up when I feel the weight of the world crashing down. You are my angel, thank you!

Finally, to my friends, I want to acknowledge each of you who has ever taken your time to read one of these writings prior to this publication. I've asked so many of you for your feedback, and you've graciously provided it. Thank you so very much! *God* Bless You!

I love you all and appreciate your support over these past thirteen years.

ABOUT THE AUTHOR

Jason grew up in Denver, Colorado before moving to Fort Collins to attend Colorado State University. While at CSU, Jason played football earning both academic and athletic accolades, and he received an undergraduate degree in Speech and Communications. After graduating, he re-enrolled and completed a graduate studies program in Computer Information Systems obtaining a Master of Science and Business Administration degree. Upon graduation, Jason spent time working in real estate, before returning to his alma-mater to coach football for two seasons. He then transitioned away from the sports world and into emergency services, becoming first a police officer and later a fire firefighter. Since becoming a firefighter, Jason has written several articles for national firefighting publications. Along the way, Jason cofounded *Guardian, LLC*, a company designed to teach leadership in emergency situations to families and businesses.

Made in the USA
Coppell, TX
11 August 2020

32978057R00094